Mail Order and Direct Response

THE NO NONSENSE LIBRARY

No Nonsense Career Guides
Managing Time
No Nonsense Management
How to Choose a Career
How to Re-enter the Workforce
How to Write a Resume
Power Interviewing
Succeeding with Difficult People

No Nonsense Financial Guides
Managing Credit and Credit Cards
Investing in Mutual Funds
Investing in the Stock Market
Investing in Tax Free Bonds
Understanding Money Market Funds
Investing in IRAs
Investing in Treasury Bills
Managing Your Stock Portfolio
Understanding Investing
How to Plan and Invest for Your Retirement
How to Buy a Home
The Truth About Mortgages

No Nonsense Success Guide
Starting a Business in Your Home
Mail Order and Direct Response

No Nonsense Health Guides

No Nonsense reference Guides

No Nonsense Parenting Guides

NO NONSENSE SUCCESS GUIDE™

MAIL ORDER

A N D

DIRECT RESPONSE

TONYA BOLDEN

Copyright © 1994 by Longmeadow Press

Published by Longmeadow Press, 201 High Ridge Road, Stamford, CT 06904. All rights reserved. No part of this book may be reproduced or utilized in any form or by any means, electronic or mechanical, including photocopying, recording or by any information storage and retrieval system, without permission in writing from the Publisher. Longmeadow Press and the Colophon are registered trademarks.

Cover design by Kelvin P. Oden

ISBN: 0681-45228-5

Library of Congress Cataloging-in-Publication Data
Bolden, Tonya.
    Mail-order and direct response/Tonya Bolden.
        p. cm — (No nonsense success guide)
    1. Mail-order business. I. Title. II. Series.
HF5466.B67 1994
658.8'72—dc20   93-35671
                                                         CIP

Printed in United States of America

First Edition

0 9 8 7 6 5 4 3 2 1

CONTENTS

INTRODUCTION

Every day when you open your mailbox, you find it chock-full of envelopes. The senders are people you don't know. The postmarks are from all across the country. Inside the envelopes you find orders (and payments in full!)—orders you, of course, fill and ship ASAP. Before long your satisfied customers are reordering your wares on a fairly regular basis and new customers are coming in just as quickly. After a while you need part-time help and you have reason to believe it won't be too long before you'll be needing a full-timer or two. And so your business booms. Month after month. Year after year. Your volume ever growing, your profits ever increasing. In a few years' time you have the luscious option of continuing to make money hand over fist or kicking back and retiring—as a multimillionaire!

As fantasies go this isn't a bad one to have—as long as you understand that it is a goal but not a guarantee of what can happen should you decide to get into the mail-order business.

If you are serious about getting into the mail-order business, you must be willing to ask your fantasy a lot of questions. Such as:

How did I decide on my product?
How did people find about it?
What compelled people to buy?
How did I fill the orders?
How did I keep track of all the business?
How much money did it take to start the business?
How many hats did I have to wear?
How did I stay out of trouble with the Feds and other agencies on the lookout for corrupt mail-order operators?

When you're prepared to deal with these questions and the dozens of others to which they give rise, you'll know you're ready to deal in mail order and get working on making that fantasy come true.

This book will provide you with the basic information you'll need in order to decide whether or not the mail-order business ought to be your business. Should the answer turn out to be a resounding "Yes!," you'll also have general guidelines and tips for starting out on the right foot.

Mail Order and
Direct Response

O N E

MAIL ORDER'S MAGIC

I f beings from another planet were to ask you, "What is this thing called mail order?," you could hand them the following passage from the Federal Trade Commission (FTC) 1975 document *Mail Order Merchandise* and feel confident that you had given them the gist of it.

"Mail order sales" refers to a marketing method whereby orders are solicited for goods which are to be ordered by mail. Some of the means by which orders are solicited include magazine and newspaper advertisements, catalogs, direct mail solicitations and telephone solicitations. While the method of payment may be cash, check, money order, credit card or debit of the buyer's account, in most instances payment is made at the time of ordering. A variety of goods are offered in this manner

including books, records, wearing apparel, home furnishings, novelty items, magazines, and nursery items.

Less mobile consumers especially, including the elderly, the sick or those living in remote or rural areas
shop in this manner as a matter of convenience. Others
do so because of possible savings or the variety or
uniqueness of goods offered.

There are about 6,000 firms in the mail order industry
with sales estimated at over 40 billion dollars annually.

If you wanted to bring the beings a little more up to date on
the matter, you could add that in recent years credit-card
wielding consumers have come to expect the option of
ordering merchandise by phone—and very recently, by
fax. Also, that since the 1970s the number of mail-order
businesses, and that the industry's estimated sales have
more than doubled.

Yes, mail order is a multibillion-dollar industry. Companies enjoying a piece of the pie include heavies such as
Time-Life Books, the Franklin Mint, Fingerhut, and Land's
End, which pull in millions, as well as smaller outfits that
can boast of profits of several hundred thousand dollars
and tiny ones that aren't one bit ashamed of the $30,000,
$40,000, or $50,000 they're bringing in.

The amazing thing about the mail-order industry is that
as crowded as it is, there's always room for one more. The
reasons are many. For one, mail-order selling and buying
are an American tradition. Second, because Americans are
busier than ever before—working, studying, playing—we
have less time for in-the-store shopping. Also, Americans
are *serious* consumers. We buy more stuff than we need,
more stuff than we know what to do with, and with the
availability of credit cards (especially those with "convenience" checks), we are buying more stuff than we can
actually afford. The Achilles heel presents mail-order operators with golden opportunities.

Making the most of these opportunities requires understanding what drives people to buy. As you know, the majority of spending that most folks do is not to meet their needs but to satisfy their wants. These wants are things that will, they hope, enable them to pursue pleasure and avoid pain. More specifically, most people want to be:

- physically attractive
- healthy and physically fit
- financially fit (earn more; save more)
- smarter
- safe
- saved from boredom (to have adventure, fun, excitement)
- Loved—or at least respected—by others.

It is important to keep these basic wants in mind, because understanding what makes people tick will help you in the decision-making process on everything from product selection and sales pitch to advertising venue and filling orders.

Understanding why people buy by mail is equally important, if for no other reason than that it'll be a constant reminder that as a mail-order operator, yes, you do have a reason for being—one that's not solely based on the chance to exploit people's wants. While mail-order shopping doesn't give people the opportunity to experience merchandise in the flesh (and thereby make a more informed decision before making the purchase), for many people this advantage of store shopping pales in comparison with the advantages of shopping by mail. The most powerful reasons many consumers are motivated to shop by mail include:

- **Convenience.** Shopping by mail means shopping when you want to. For people with very hectic lives this is a precious option—and even more so for the elderly, infirm, and disabled, for whom in-the-store shopping would be a major chore, if not an impossibility.

- **Time savings.** Mail-order shopping reduces shopping time down to the time it takes to select the merchandise and mail or phone in the order. This is particularly appealing to people who don't have access to a shopping center and to those who hate waiting in line. Mail-order shopping—at least the browsing part—is also a time saver in that it allows people to do two things at once. You can, for example, shop while you sit under a hair dryer, take a bath, eat, or wait in line, and you can shop during your commute (as long as you're not driving).

- **Peace.** Mail-order shopping is pressure-free. There's no salesperson breathing down shoppers' necks or interrupting their browsing with "Can I help you?" or an unsolicited sales pitch. And given that these days far too many salespeople are rude, lazy, and ignorant about the merchandise they handle, many shoppers find little need for them anyway and so don't feel they're missing anything when they shop by mail.

- **Privacy.** Nobody's perfect and everybody knows it. And yet people are constantly measuring themselves against some mythical, media-hyped ideal and are very self-conscious about their imperfection. Hence, buying remedies and cover-ups for their "problems" by mail spares them the embarrassment they would feel if they purchased these goods in a store in front of "everybody." In short, people prefer to by things like shoe lifts, nose-hair scissors, and anti-baldness products by mail.

- **Fun.** It may sound a little silly to some, but in actuality mail-order shopping can add a bit of adventure and intrigue to an otherwise humdrum life. It gives people something to look forward to, and when an order arrives, something of a present to unwrap.

- **Money savings.** Unless an item is extremely novel, exotic, or otherwise hard to find, people expect to save money when they do business by mail. And this isn't an

4

unreasonable expectation, since most mail-order outfits don't have the kind of overhead that stores have and can afford not to mark up an item as much as in order to make a profit.

• **Access.** People who don't live in or near a big city don't have access to a lot of products that big-city dwellers take for granted.

A mail-order business is a good proposition for an aspiring entrepreneur. It's a low-investment/quick-results business. This is not to say that a mail-order business isn't a gamble. All businesses are. But compared with other businesses, it doesn't require a lot of start-up money: in many cases, only a few thousand dollars. Neither does it require years of investigation or formal education to launch: six months to a year of research and preparation—reading, thinking, and perhaps attending a seminar or two—should do it. And unless you are extremely dense, it won't take you forever to know whether or not you're truly in business or whether you should fold. Finally, two of the most obvious advantages of a mail-order business for the novice entrepreneur is that it's so easy to operate from home and it doesn't require a full-time commitment—ever! This means you don't have to give up your job to get into it. And if you have small children to care for or other familial responsibilities, you can have a business and fulfill present or ongoing obligations.

Should you have doubts that you can make big money in mail order, just do a little digging and you'll find that many a one-person, low-budget operation has grown into a major enterprise. That is, not only is there room in the mail-order business for another little guy or gal, but there's room for the new kid on the block to make major money. In his book *Building a Mail Order Business,* William A. Cohen cites a number of examples that bear witness to this fact. One of the stories he tells is of Richard Thalheimer, who in the late 1970s recognized the popularity of the

Seiko chronograph watch and found a source for a similar but cheaper watch, which he proceeded to sell by mail. From this little acorn grew the major mail-order company the Sharper Image, which has mailed out more than 280 million catalogues to date, and in 1993 netted approximately $150 million from its catalogue and retail store sales. Another story Cohen recounts is of a young wife and mother named Lillian. In 1951, in her efforts to make a little money on the side, she latched on to the idea of selling personalized belts and purses and set up shop on her kitchen table. She's better known today as Lillian Vernon, whose company's annual sales are $175 million, with a catalogue circulation of more than 140 million.

These are but two of the hundreds of once small-time mail-order operators who made it big-time. Their recipe for success may have included a dash of luck, but the main ingredient was good old-fashioned hard work—not to mention the right attitude and aptitude for being an entrepreneur, which is the subject of the next chapter.

TWO

ON BEING AN ENTREPRENEUR

Having your own business, no matter how small, can be a truly wondrous and exhilarating thing. It allows you to explore and manifest your potential and develop new skills as few jobs can. If you plan and manage your enterprise right, you can also make more money than you could on your present career path. Plus, you won't have to live in fear of being fired. Clearly, having your own business can be very rewarding on many levels. But it is also very serious business. It is a major undertaking that will demand more of you than you can possibly imagine at the outset. Learning all you can about it certainly helps, but there's nothing like living it. In short, a business can make you or break you. And this is why before you go any further with your education in the mail-order business, you need to take

7

time to really consider whether or not you have what it takes to start and operate a business.

YOUR MOTIVATION

The most sane and sensible reason for starting a business is that you have a viable product. Other factors may be the spark that moves you to investigate the possibility, but they should not be the determining factor. Let's look at some of the sparks and their pitfalls.

• **The Job Blues.** Do you hate your job? If so, remember that anger and frustration can severely cloud your judgment. When you're operating out of these emotions, you're likely to make bad decisions.

• **The Boss Blues.** In many cases when people say, "I want to be my own boss!," what they're really saying is "I hate my boss!" And often, if they move to another position or another place of employment and find themselves working under someone with whom they get along, the urge to boss themselves around subsides.

• **Unemployment.** The loss of a job will certainly compel a person to consider a lot of options. But if you've just lost your job, you might not be in the best frame of mind to launch a business. Also, unless you have a little nest egg to fall back on, where are you going to get the money to start a business and to live on while you're waiting for the business to turn a profit?

• **The Money Blues.** Even a part-time mail-order business requires some start-up capital. This means that in order to make money you'll need to spend money. Also, inasmuch as most businesses do not show a net profit before the first year of operation, if you need to make more money yesterday, a better-paying job or an extra job might be the most profitable thing to do for the immediate future.

- **Time Control.** A mail-order business will allow you more flexibility in scheduling the affairs of your life, but it won't give you more free time. And if you start it while you're holding down another job, you won't be seeing much free time for a good long while.

- **Fulfillment.** A business will keep you busy but it won't give you true contentment and a feeling of self-worth. If you're operating under the illusion that a business will boost your self-esteem, be forewarned that high self-esteem is a prerequisite, not a consequence, of succeeding in a business.

- **Fashion.** Home basing it is rather in vogue these days. But if you join the crowd, simply because you deem it the "in" thing to do, you're setting yourself up for the possibility of a maddening experience.

Each of the above or a combination of them might be just the thing to get you *thinking* about starting your own business, but they shouldn't be the thing that motivates your *doing* it. If you let your emotions lead, nine times out of ten they will mislead you. First and foremost they may cause you to delude yourself about the viability of a product.

YOUR PERSONALITY

Not everyone is cut out to be an entrepreneur. And while there is no acid test for what makes one person more suitable for running a business than another, there are some indicators. For starters, an entrepreneur should be:

- self-disciplined
- diligent
- energetic
- able to take constructive criticism
- aggressive
- self-confident

- mentally mobile
- perspicacious

If this sounds like you, then you have the makings of an entrepreneur. If it doesn't, then running your own business might be risky business indeed. Of course, people who don't have these characteristics but have their own business may come to mind and you might be tempted to think, "Well, if they can, why can't I?" Before you start grasping at straws, remember that very often people who have absolutely no business brains or guts are mere figureheads or fronts, with other partners pulling their strings and running the show. In other cases, the person may have at least been smart enough to staff the enterprise with smarter, more competent people. Of course when you're talking about a one-person operation, there's no one else to take up and make up for your slack.

To further assess whether or not you have the personality for running a business, take the self-employment aptitude test. Check "Yes" or "No" based on how you are as a rule.

	YES	NO
• Are you basically lazy?	_____	_____
• Are you allergic to scutwork?	_____	_____
• Are you unorganized?*	_____	_____
• Do you tend to cut and run at the mere hint of adversity?	_____	_____
• Are you easily influenced by others?	_____	_____
• Are you forgetful?	_____	_____
• Are you a procrastinator?	_____	_____

*Remember that an unorganized person doesn't know the meaning of the word *order*, whereas a disorganized person may have things temporarily out of order. So if you sometimes let things get messy but then can make order out of chaos and get all systems going, you're not *un*organized.

- Are you naive or gullible?   _____ _____
- Are you highly panic-prone?   _____ _____
- Are you very impulsive?   _____ _____
- Do you work best with super-
  vision?   _____ _____
- Are you a spendthrift?   _____ _____
- Do you stress out easily?   _____ _____
- Do you have a tendency to be
  dishonest?   _____ _____
- Are you more concerned with
  style than with substance?   _____ _____
- Do you have a short attention
  span?   _____ _____
- Do you have a tendency to be
  irresponsible?   _____ _____
- Do you daydream a lot?   _____ _____
- Are you a people pleaser?   _____ _____
- Do you admire Don Quixote
  more than, say, Paul Bunyan?   _____ _____

If you checked a lot of yes's and you could only claim a few of the attributes listed earlier, then the odds are you won't be able to make a successful go of a business. There is, however, the possibility of your changing the odds. If you can be realistic about your shortcomings, you may well be able to make the behavior and attitude modifications that would render you more suitable for entrepreneurship.

YOUR MENTAL HEALTH

Even if you have the makings of an entrepreneur *par excellence*, if you are at present a mental and emotional

11

wreck you should tend to your inner well-being before you pursue a business. Any business—even a part-time one—is emotionally draining and mentally straining. Start-up is particularly stressful, even if you are, on some level, loving every minute of it. Granted, a new project may be just the thing to get you "back in the saddle." But then again, it could well be the straw that breaks the camel's back.

YOUR PHYSICAL HEALTH

A mail-order business can be very labor-intensive. It can involve lots of toting, lifting, and miscellaneous moving about. Unless you will have some part-time help, whatever you can't do won't get done. Remember, you'll not only be the boss but the staff as well. Physical limitations or disabilities don't necessarily disqualify you for a mail-order business, but they do mean that you will have to think through ways to work around them so that they won't be a hindrance.

YOUR FINANCIAL HEALTH

Counting the financial cost of starting a mail-order business will be taken up in Chapter 9. At this point there's no way for you to ascertain whether or not you can afford to start a business. You can, however, determine whether or not you can afford to investigate the possibility. One of the keys to a successful launch is thorough research and planning—a.k.a. doing your homework. For this you will need money for such things as phone calls, books, periodicals and other materials, a course or two, and, perhaps, sampling your competition's wares. One by one these things might seem like chump change, but they add up to several hundred dollars. So if your finances are in a shambles, you should probably hold off.

YOUR FAMILY

If you have a family, be sure to consider your spouse and/or children in your decision-making process because your business will affect their lives. If nothing else, you'll be asking them to give up a little bit of you, but you'll probably also be asking them to make some adjustments with regard to household chores, expenditures, lifestyle, and living room. If there's a chance that your embarking on a business could be very disruptive, you'd be wise to abandon the idea for the time being. Remember, ideally you want to start your business with the support and understanding of your family. After all, chances are you will need their help.

YOUR SPATIAL RELATIONS

You may not need a great deal of space to start your business, but you will need some. Yes, lots of people boast of beginning their business from the kitchen table or nightstand, but that doesn't work for everybody. If you have an extra room, or part or all of an attic or basement that's vacant (or can be easily made so), then you're in luck. If you barely have room to breathe in your present abode, bringing a business into it may drive you up the wall. As you assess your living quarters, remember that you'll need work surfaces, space for equipment, and room for supplies and inventory.

This chapter wasn't intended to discourage you—unless, of course, you have none of what it takes. If this is true, and you can't see yourself doing anything to change the situation, you should be happy to have come to this realization sooner as opposed to later.

If you have some of what it takes, there's hope. Taking a holistic look at yourself and your circumstances and 'fessing up to your problem points means that you at least know what areas of your life you'll need to work on to increase your chances of success—whether it's working some overtime to get your finances in better shape so that you can afford to do your homework properly, or whether it's to get yourself on a stress-reduction regimen so you'll have the mental and emotional stamina to do it. Acknowledging your limitations or inadequacies will also help you make better decisions on the nature and structure of your business. For example, if you have a great product idea but don't have the best business sensibilities, you know that you need to look for a partner with a business head and the skills to match. Similarly, if you've been toying with the idea of selling either twelve-ounce or ten-pound widgets, confronting how bad your back really is should solve the dilemma.

THREE

PRODUCT SELECTION

To find the mail-order product that's right for you, you must first get a rein on what is *verboten*. You'll then need to browse through the realm of possibilities, do a little brainstorming on your own, and get a handle on the factors to consider when making the final decision. Even if you're pretty much sold on what you want to sell, don't skip this chapter. It may lead you to an even better idea, or at least help you reevaluate yours.

THE FORBIDDENS

While there are thousands of things that can be sold by mail, there are some things that are strictly forbidden. They are:

• **The Dangerous.** An item may be legal to have in your possession, but if it is undeniably or potentially hazardous, sending it through the mail may be illegal, and hence it would have to be ruled out as a mail-order product. So take note of the following advisory from the United States Postal Service (USPS) pamphlet *How to Prepare and Wrap Packages:*

It is illegal to send through the U.S. Mail any article, composition or material which may kill or injure another person, or obstruct mail service or damage property. Harmful matter includes, but is not limited to:
  • All kinds of poison or matter containing poison;
  • All poisonous animals, most poisonous insects, all poisonous reptiles, and all kinds of snakes and spiders;
  • All disease germs or scabs; and
  • All explosives, flammable material, dangerous machines, and mechanical, chemical or other devices or compositions which may catch fire or explode.

There are also legal restrictions on the mailing of:
  • Radioactive material;
  • Firearms, knives, and sharp instruments;
  • Drugs and narcotics;
  • Other controlled substances as defined by Federal law and related Federal regulations.

Certain potentially harmful or dangerous articles and substances may be mailed if special packaging and labeling requirements are met.

Chances are you would never think of building a mail-order business on anything hazardous. But to make doubly sure you don't, you should review the USPS publication *Acceptance of Hazardous, Restricted or Perishable Matter.*

• **Pornography.** It is illegal to sell pornographic materials—audio, visual, or print—via mail. If you already have or should come up with a product that could possibly be deemed pornographic or obscene, you'd do well to consult an attorney.

• **New Drugs.** Even if you or someone you know has discovered a medical remedy, you cannot sell it without permission from the Food and Drug Administration (FDA).

• **Lotteries.** Only state-owned and -operated lotteries can be conducted through the mail. As the USPS booklet *A Consumer's Guide to Postal Crime Prevention* states:

> Federal law makes it a crime to mail letters or circulars containing lottery material . . . including tickets or forms claiming to represent tickets, chances, shares, or interests in lotteries.

As it goes on to explain, the three elements that make a lottery illegal are:

1. A *payment* is required (cash or money order).
2. A *prize* is offered (money or something of value).
3. A return on investment depends on *chance* (all recipients will participate).

There is a fine line between a lottery and a contest or sweepstakes. Should you ever contemplate one of these, be sure to discuss the matter with an attorney so that you don't cross that line.

• **"Chain Gangs."** This is a variation of the old-fashioned chain letter where people were urged to circulate the letter (sometimes along with a dollar or two) to avoid some personal disaster or receive some metaphysical or material boon. The chain letter as mail-order scheme is different in that recipients are usually roped into buying some bit of nothing that passes as major information (most often it's a get-rich-quick formula). In theory, if the recipients follow the instructions laid out in the letter, they will have scores of people sending them money for copies of this material. In reality, the only person who ever makes any kind of money is the person who starts the chain. Although many proponents of this kind of "business" maintain that it's as legitimate as other forms of multilevel-marketing enterprises, the Feds don't agree and condemn it as unethical and illegal.

THE POSSIBILITIES

The perfectly legal and potentially very profitable mail-order ideal merchandise would fill a book. Below are some of the strongest categories of mail-order goods.

Artwork: For many people an environment (home, workplace) without a little bit of art is like a day without sunshine. Such people are always looking for something to adorn their walls, desktops, shelves, coffee tables, and other surfaces on which they can place a work of art. When you think art, don't just think originals. Reproductions sell very well. While people ego-trip over owning a one-of-a-kind work of art, the more expensive the piece the less likely they are to buy it through the mail unless it is offered on a trial basis.

Audiofare: Listening to music is one of the most popular pastimes. And while what people listen to may be mostly music, it's not only that. People who are semi-literate, slow readers, or nonreaders relish opportunities to access information and entertainment (e.g., books on tape) through the "eargate" as opposed to the "eyegate."

Auto-Care Products: Items in this category range from the things that will make a vehicle run better and more safely to things that'll make it look and smell better to all those little accessories that make driving more comfortable and in-the-car tasks more manageable.

Books: Books have always been a strong mail-order item. You can sell one or a series of books that you or someone else has authored and self-published. Or you could sell a line of hard-to-find or out-of-print books. You could also specialize in a particular category of books like business, children's, gardening, self-help, or fiction and nonfiction about people of a certain ethnic group or religious belief.

Cleaning Supplies. For the home and the office.

Clothing: Outerwear and underwear. For men, women, and children. If you carry merchandise that is one-size-fits-all or that is sized small, medium, large, and so forth, you increase your chances of sales and reduce the number of returns. Sized clothing sells, but selling it requires more extensive (and hence, more expensive) promotional material.

Clothing Accessories: Belts, purses, shawls, scarves, ties, and all the other stuff people use to jazz up and recycle their wardrobe.

Collectibles. Coins, stamps, miniatures, memorabilia. Not everything that people collect is precious to the world at large. Value is in the eye of the beholder, and so one person's trash may be another person's treasure.

Food: Gourmet, specialty, "secret recipe," and health-food items will obviously sell better than products readily and widely available on supermarket shelves. But bear in mind that food and beverages require special packaging and handling. So if you are considering dealing in perishables, you should start with items that aren't too fragile and don't perish too quickly.

Gifts: Items that classify as all-occasion gifts sell well, but you'll have more success with items that have a motif or design that speaks to major religious and secular days of celebration, such as Christmas, Hanukkah, Kwanzaa, Mother's Day, Father's Day, and rites of passage in the cycle of life such as marriage, graduation, the birth of a child, a wedding anniversary, or a bar or bas mitzvah. Remember that very often what can make an ordinary item gift-worthy is the presentation and packaging.

Health and Beauty Aids: Given the American obsession with looks and living as long as possible, is it any wonder that this is a strong category for mail-order sales? This category includes cosmetics; perfume; vitamins; tonics; toiletries for face, body, and hair; and all sorts of things that make people feel and appear more beautiful and vital. It also includes tools, applicators, and other gizmos used in personal hygiene and grooming regimens.

Hobby Helps: Think of all the creative things that people do in their spare time—ceramics, drawing, cooking, gardening (indoor and outdoor), model building, music making, needlecrafts, painting, photography, woodworking—and you'll see that there are hundreds of products they need to "do their thing."

Home Furnishings and Housewares: From kitchen and bathroom gadgets to tableware. From small-ticket items like curtains, throw pillows, and waste baskets to more expensive items like area rugs and minor-league furniture. Remember that people are always looking for easy and inexpensive ways to spruce up their environment, organize their possessions, and simplify household tasks.

Information: We live in the information age and people can't seem to get enough of it—in the form of lists, data, tips, guides, and other printed matter to short to qualify as a book.

Jewelry: Curious and eclectic pieces of adornment are likely to sell better than the run-of-the-mill, unless your prices are wonderfully low.

Novelties: This is a catch-all term for magic tricks, jokes, and other nonsensicals. People go in for bits of silliness, and the less expensive an item is, the more people will indulge their craving for a little whimsy.

Officewares: There's money to be made in both garden-variety, state-of-the-art, and otherwise peculiar office supplies.

Pet-Care Products: People with pets and discretionary income are very likely to pamper their animals with grooming products, toys, special bedding, and even clothing.

Religious Items: This category includes jewelry, knick-knacks, novelties and household ornaments with religious symbols, sacred books, and items used in public and private devotionals.

Sporting Goods and Exercise Equipment: For indoor and outdoor action in the winter, spring, summer, and fall. For fitness freaks who shape up at home, in the office, and in the great outdoors.

Stationery: From greeting cards and note cards to postcards and calendars (wall and desk), and more, stationery has been a strong seller.

Toys and Games: Dolls, action figures, jigsaw puzzles, playing cards, board games, mind teasers. Remember that playing isn't just kid stuff. Many adults spend big money on things that bring out the child in them.

Although most of the what sells through the mail are tangibles, some products are services. Examples: accounting, bookbinding, correspondence courses, financial planning, framing, menu planning, photofinishing, writing, and editing. Because rendering a service by mail is generally a very involved process, don't consider it if you haven't already done so. If you have toyed with the idea, think it through very well. A service is a harder sell. Most people prefer to have face-to-face contact with their service providers.

IDEA SHOPPING

Here are six courses of action to consider in your product search.

• **Go to the trade shows, expos, and inventors' shows.** At these venues you'll get an eyeful of products about to come out on the market, items already being sold, and some that are looking for someone to market them. When you attend these events, don't look only for a ready-made product; think about items that might complement or accessorize a product that shows signs of becoming a hot commodity. If you don't know what kinds of merchandise events are on the horizon for your area, get in touch with your chamber of commerce.

• **Visit flea markets.** Here you will get a sense of some of the eclectic things people are selling and buying. Since a lot of people sell handcrafted and homemade goods at flea markets, you may find an artist or artisan who would be interested in becoming your supplier or perhaps going into a partnership with you.

• **Read ads.** Magazines, newspapers, and other varieties of periodicals that carry ads for mail-order products are great sources for ideas. Seeing what other people are selling will give you a feel for what's hot and what's not. As a rule, if you never see ads for a product you frequently see in stores, chances are that's because it doesn't sell well through the mail. Of course it could be that no one has ever figured out how to make the winning pitch. If you're convinced that such is the case, then you should "go for it," understanding full well that you're in for a challenge.

• **Study trends.** Do a little reflecting on what's going on in the world in terms of how people live, work, study, and play. Think, too, about changing sensibilities about relationships, the environment, diet, politics, and so forth.

Every ethos, every movement, every major happening opens the door for new products or takeoffs on the old. Just think about all the merchandise the jogging craze brought into our lives! Or, more recently, the recycling ethic and laws.

• **Talk to people.** Ask friends, relatives, and associates what kind of merchandise they are most likely to buy through the mail, what products they'd never buy through the mail, and what kinds of things they wish they could get by mail.

• **Read your mail.** Your mailbox is the most-at-hand and one of the best repositories of ideas. Instead of summarily discarding your junk mail and the pounds of catalogues that come your way, sift through this material for both inspiration and insight as to what others are selling by mail (and hence a bandwagon you could jump on).

THE PROCESS OF ELIMINATION

If you're not already sold on what to sell, sorting through all the possibilities can be quite frustrating and mind-boggling. But the process of elimination isn't as difficult as you might think. It's simply a matter a thinking things through. Here are ten dos that'll help you choose.

• **Choose a product that is easy to acquire.** The best product is one that you create or manufacture because it eliminates reliance on suppliers who could "jam" you should their business come up against disaster. If you aren't your own supplier, ideally you should be able to get the product from more than one supplier, even if you end up using only one. The point: don't put all your eggs in one basket. Furthermore, you don't want to have to go through extraordinary measures to acquire a product, because in all likelihood such will cost you more money, time, and headaches. So if you're considering a product that would have to be imported from, say, Azerbaijan, be sure to count all the costs of getting the goods.

One idea is to query companies about merchandise they have discontinued but still have stock on and see if they'd allow you to take this merchandise off their hands. The reasoning behind this suggestion is that you can often find very viable products at almost giveaway prices. The problem with it is that if you are successful at moving this merchandise, once you've done so you'll have to hunt up another "steal."

• **Choose a product that packages and ships well.** The less complex packaging and extra-care handling an item requires, the lower your cost to fill orders and the fewer headaches you'll have to even anticipate. This is not to say that you shouldn't consider a fragile, perishable, or somehow unwieldy item but only that you'd do well to think long and hard about the worst-case scenarios such as spoilage, breakage, and "crushage" and how you can prepare against them.

• **Choose a product that appeals to people's basic wants.** The more, the better. For example, if a product can make people feel or look more attractive and it saves them a little money, its selling potential will be all the greater. If you have several totally unrelated products or lines of products in mind, revisit the list of wants and mail-order shoppers' motivations discussed in Chapter 1 and see which product or line satisfies the most wants.

• **Choose a product that isn't widely available in stores.** Relatively speaking, that is. The unavailability of an item in a store will certainly be a strong selling point. Also, the less available it is, the less competition you have. However, the availability factor may be irrelevant, depending on the market you target. What's widely available to a big-city dweller may be a rare commodity for someone in a rural area. Moreover, the availability of an item in big cities and small towns alike doesn't help prison inmates, shut-ins, or others who are for various reasons unable to visit stores.

• **Choose a product that is in some way unique.** There should be something out-of-the-ordinary about your product. One way of making a product unique is to offer it personalized. You can also make an old product new by simply putting a religious, ethnic, or "consciousness" spin on it. The T-shirt is a classic example. While coming up with something that is new under the sun is a mail-order operator's dream, putting a twist on something tried and true is a lot less risky and sometimes a lot cheaper than taking something that's never been seen or conceived and getting it to market. For unless you can maintain an exclusive on your innovation, inside of a few months or a year of your getting it to market, others will have copied you. If the copycats only come up with cheap imitations of your "real thing," your business won't be as much in jeopardy. But should they, in fact, devise a better mousetrap, you will surely lose your corner on the market.

• **Choose a product that can be conveyed in a few words or in a little bit of space.** The less time, energy, and supporting materials it takes for people to "get" what you're selling, the better. People don't buy what they don't understand. And the more elaborate a presentation your product requires, the most costly it'll be to promote that product.

• **Choose a product that's based on a trend instead of one based on a fad.** Some people have made killings on fads, but fad-driven business can be disastrous business, because if you don't have excellent instincts you may either jump on the bandwagon too late or stay on it too long. (Remember, you don't want to end up with the Nehru jacket of the 1990s). It can also be exhausting, because you'll have to be ready with another fad item before interest in your first one fizzles out.

• **Choose a product you know (or can easily learn) something about.** You don't have to be an engineer to sell pocket calculators, but a rudimentary understanding of how they work wouldn't hurt. For one, you'll be less likely to be duped by a supplier. Also, the more you know about something, the better you'll be able to sell it.

• **Choose a product you feel positive about.** The better you feel about the product, the easier it will be to sell.

• **Choose a product that will have mass appeal.** If you can reasonably see your "thingamajig" in the hands or homes of men and women ages twenty-five to fifty across racial, socioeconomic, and other lines, your volume potential will be much larger than if the product could only be of interest to Tlingit women with small children. This isn't to say that you can't do a healthy amount of business with a product that will appeal only to a particular group of people, for you most certainly can, provided the special-interest product has a natural customer base on more than a few hundred people. It is especially crucial to have a broad customer base if you will be selling a one-shot product—that is, an item that will last a customer a lifetime.

One of the most important questions you can ask of a product under consideration is "Who's going to buy you?" Having a vague idea or hope that a product will appeal to "a lot of people" won't cut it. You have to be able to identify the market so that you will be able to determine whether it'll be worth your while to try to reach that market. Seeing your market means knowing what your potential customers look like in terms of age, gender, race or ethnicity, marital status, geographical location, income, education, occupation, religion, and other matters of life and living.

Because your product is the foundation of your business, there's no room for rashness—only for careful and objective thought. Product selection isn't an exact science. It basically comes down to common sense and the honest answer to three questions:

- Is anyone really going to want what you're selling?
- Will product acquisition be problematic?
- Will you be able to sell a product for a lot more than it'll cost you to acquire the product, promote the product, and get the product in the mail?

FOUR

THE OFFER

The offer is the sum total of things that make a product and the purchasing process an appealing proposition. Some contend that in the mail-order success ratio, it's 60 percent the product and 40 percent the offer; others, that it's 50/50. While people may quibble about the ratio, it's an undisputed fact that the offer is a major factor in winning customers over.

THE PRICE

What you charge for your product is the cornerstone of your offer. Unless the price feels right to people, they won't give your product a first look. Many people set the price of their product by totaling up what it costs to get the product in the mail to the consumer and multiplying that figure by 3 or 4. This multiplication is called the "markup." To gauge the sanity of this price, they then take a look at how much others are charging for the same or similar item. Here's a hypothetical scenario of a price setting in action.

Mr. X's product is the monogrammed kryptonite widget. He gets the widgets for $60 a case (24 in a case) plus $5 per case for shipping and handling and will have them monogrammed at a shop down the street for 50 cents apiece. He'll ship the goods via third-class mail in padded bags that cost $12 per hundred. His per-widget in-the-mail cost is:

His cost per unit	$2.50
Delivery from supplier	.21
Monogramming	.50
Packaging	.12
Postage (average)	1.23
TOTAL	$4.56

Using the standard industry markup range, Mr. X figured on setting his price somewhere between $14 and $18. But before making a final decision, he took a look at what the market could bear.

Had he found that other companies were selling monogrammed kryptonite widgets for $20, he might have decided to sell his for $17 or $18 and thereby appeal to consumer's save-money mentality. Or he could have opted to run with the pack and charged $20, knowing that he'd have to come up with a super pitch to make people buy his widgets over those of his competitors. And had he discovered that his competitors' widgets are made of a low-grade kryptonite, he might then have decided to sell his for $21 or $22 with every intention of pointing out the superiority of his product.

What Mr. X, in fact, discovered was that he's the only retailer of these widgets in the Western world (his supplier's only other customer is in Bora Bora), and he realized that if his widgets captured the hearts of consumers he could charge anything he wanted. To find out what that might be, he placed ads in several publications. In these ads his sale price was $30, and within one month his ads brought in 50 orders. He then ran the same ad in the same publications offering his wares at the reduced price of $25. This time he received 200 orders within a month's time. Mr. X decided to hold his price at $25.

As this hypothetical scenario shows, there are a lot of variables when it comes to setting a price. But the bottom line is that your price must be profitable for you and attractive to consumers. This may mean charging a little less than you'd like in order to do the kind of volume that will keep you in business over the long haul. Remember, too, that while bargains are strong sellers, too cheap might not pay. Not because you won't make a profit, but because many consumers are suspicious of anything that's too cheap.

The Money-Back Guarantee

Mail-order shipping is definitely an act of faith, because people never really know what they're getting until they've paid their money. Hence, offering prospective customers a money-back guarantee is the ethical thing to do. It is also the practical thing to do, since many periodicals don't take advertisements from companies that don't offer a guarantee, and a lot of shoppers prefer to buy from ones that do.

There are different kinds of guarantees: from the seven-day, the thirty-day, and the one-year to the high-stakes, double-your-money-back. You can make your guarantee unconditional—"No questions asked"—or contingent upon product failure or defect. Offering a guarantee should not be problematic if your product lives up to the claims you make about it and the expectations of reasonable customers. The more solid your product, the stronger the guarantee you should make. If you're already starting to cringe at the thought of returns consider this: Most people do not bother asking for their money back unless they are deeply dissatisfied with a product; rather, they generally decide to "get you back" by never purchasing from you again and encouraging others to do likewise. In the event that you find that over 15 percent of your customers take you up on your money-back offer, you'll know there really is something wrong with your product.

THE METHOD OF PAYMENT

How people have to pay for the goods is a definite factor in their decision to place an order. Since you cannot make everyone happy on this count, your payment program should be based on a combination of what is most expedient for you in light of your resources and what is most appropriate for your product. Your basic options are:

• **Cash.** This is the simplest. It includes "real money," money order, and check. Offering people the option of all three will get you more responses than if you offer only one of them. Granted, sending dollars through the mail is risky (and is discouraged by the post office), but if your product only costs a few dollars, people will generally take the risk. The chances of your never receiving the envelope shouldn't be that high, because people who send money through the mail usually know how to do so without attracting the attention of thieves. If you require money orders only, you're likely to discourage people from ordering, because getting a money order isn't always convenient. Payment by check is most convenient for most people. It also makes customers feel more secure about ordering, because they know that their canceled check will provide them with some documentation. Granted, accepting checks is risky business; however, you will minimize the risk if your delivery date includes time (three to five business days) for a check to clear. If you ship merchandise before the check clears it'll cost you bank charges *and* lost profit, whereas if you find out you've gotten a bad check before you ship, your loss will be limited to the bank charges.

• **"Bill Me Later."** With this payment plan, you would include the invoice with the shipment or send it out a few days after the shipment. The option of buying now and paying later will induce a great number of people to place orders—especially for higher-priced merchandise. For one thing, people are twice as likely to follow through on an impulse when they can defer payment. Moreover, having the option of ordering now and being billed later inspires shoppers with confidence that you're on the up-and-up, and gives them the comfort that if they are dissatisfied with your product they can return it and be done with you as opposed to returning it and then waiting for a refund. Obviously this payment option opens you up to rip-offs. Unfortunately, there are more than a few people out there who specialize in getting something (like your product) for nothing (they simply ignore your bill). And remember that the time and energy you'd put into pursuing payment yourself, or the cost of turning the matter over to a collection agency, will leave you no recourse other than to take the loss. Even if you only draw honest customers, remember that the bill-me-later option will require you to set up and maintain a billing system that will cost you time and money. (Bill Me Later's cousin, the installment plan, can be a similarly involved and tedious affair and should likewise only be considered for big-ticket items.)

• **C.O.D.** This is like Bill Me Later except that USPS is the collector. The downside of C.O.D. is that should your shipment come at a bad time, the customer may refuse it, in which case you're out the "to" and "return" postage, as well as the fee for C.O.D. service.

• **Credit Card.** For medium- and big-ticket items alike, many a mail-order business has boosted its sales with this option. It isn't recommended, however, for beginners with a small operation, because it's not that easy to become a credit-card merchant. Most banks and companies won't even let you get as far as filling out an application unless you've been in business for at least two years. And if you do get as far as the application process, be prepared for intense scrutiny. Because the mail-order industry is rife with fraud, banks and companies aren't as quick to take on mail-order operators as they are other kinds of businesses. There are brokers who can expedite matters, but it'll cost you several hundred to a thousand dollars more. Remember, too, that even if you do manage to become a card acceptor, a lot of customers may not even take you up on this option. With all the credit-card fraud that goes on, people are reluctant to give out their credit-card numbers to a business they've never heard of or dealt with before.

SPECIAL DELIVERY

Most mail-order shoppers are content to wait a few weeks for their merchandise. If you want to entice the anxious and last-minute shoppers, however, you should make some kind of rush delivery available. It might be next-day or two-day delivery with USPS, Federal Express, United Parcel Service, or other express courier service. Whatever it is, you should advise customers of the cost for such.

DISCOUNTS

Discounts are a powerful incentive to buy, and they come in many varieties. Among them: the quantity discount (for example, "But 3, get 1 free"); the first-time customer discount, where a flat amount or a percentage of the merchandise total is taken off; the deadline discount (X amount or percentage off for orders received by a certain date); and the second-time customer discount, where you give people something off their second order.

FREEBIES

People like to feel that their business is appreciated. One of the best ways to tell them that it *is* appreciated is to give them a little gift. The gift might be conditional—contingent upon, for example, the size of the order, or an order received by such-and-such a date, or for first-time customers only. Or customers may receive the gift with their order as a total surprise. If you do decide to give your customers some tangible thank-you, it should be something related to the merchandise. For example, if you're selling books, you might want to give bookmarks or bookplates; if stationery, a pen or marker; if yarn, a booklet of knitting tips. Your freebie shouldn't cost you too much to produce or acquire. At the same time, you shouldn't get too cheap on people. Better not to give anything than to insult people with a piece of junk.

Another kind of freebie is free shipping or a nominal charge for shipping and handling. You should consider this only if the shipping and handling aren't that costly. Or you could decide to offer free shipping and handling only for orders over $50, $100, or whatever dollars. Some people advertise "free shipping and handling" when what they've actually done is included these charges in the sale price. Free shipping and handling is when you eat the cost, not when you merely hide it from the consumer.

In many books on mail-order business, you will also come across the suggestion that you offer information as a freebie. If this information is in no way a part of your sales pitch, then that's one thing. If it is, then consumers are likely to resent your trying to pass it off as a free gift.

When structuring your offer, don't think short-term. While a super launch offer that includes a discount and a freebie may mean little or no profit, if it draws a lot of first-timer customers it will pay off in the long run— provided, of course, that you do what it takes to turn first-timers into repeat customers and/or satisfied customers who will spread the word about your product.

THE FEDERAL TRADE COMMISSION MAIL-ORDER RULE

One of the strictures your offer must abide by is this 1976 regulation, commonly referred to as the "30-Day Rule," or simply "the Rule." In a nutshell it says that you have to ship merchandise on time: either by the ship date advertised, or within 30 days of receipt of the order if no ship date was given. The Rule sounds simple, but as with all regulations it has its share of complicating details, which if overlooked could land you in court. Below is the opening passage of the Mail Order Rule proper.

In connection with mail order sales in commerce, as "commerce" is defined in the Federal Trade Commission Act, it constitutes an unfair method of competition, and an unfair or deceptive act and practice for the seller:

(a) (1) To solicit any order for the sale of merchandise to be ordered by the buyer through the mails unless, at the time of the solicitation, the seller has a reasonable basis to expect that he will be able to ship any ordered merchandise to the buyer: (i) within that time clearly and conspicuously stated in any such solicitation, or (ii) if no time is clearly and conspicuously stated, within thirty (30) days after receipt of a properly completed order from the buyer.

(2) To provide any buyer with any revised shipping

date, as provided in paragraph (b), unless, at the time any such revised shipping date is provided, the seller has a reasonable basis for making such representation regarding a definite revised shipping date.

(3) To inform any buyer that he is unable to make representation regarding the length of any delay unless (i) the seller has a reasonable basis for so informing the buyer and (ii) the seller informs the buyer of the reason or reasons for the delay.

(b) (1) Where a seller is unable to ship merchandise within the applicable time set forth in paragraph (a) (1), above, to fail to offer to the buyer, clearly and conspicuously and without prior demand, an option either to consent to a delay in shipping or to cancel his order and receive a prompt refund. Said offer shall be made within the applicable time set forth in paragraph (a) (1), but in no event later than said applicable time.

The Rule goes on for several more paragraphs that make for truly arduous reading. Luckily the FTC has produced the booklet, *A Business Guide to the Federal Trade Commission's Mail Order Rule,* which will help you better understand the Rule and thereby better abide by it. As a prospective mail-order operator, you should make it your business to get a copy of the Rule and the explanatory booklet sooner rather than later. In the meantime, the following excerpts from the booklet will give you a bit more grounding in the matter.

WHAT TO KNOW
WHEN YOU MAKE AN OFFER

When you offer to sell merchandise by mail, the Rule requires you to have a "reasonable basis" for expecting to ship within the time stated in your solicitation.

For example, if you know before advertising your products that your suppliers are on strike for several months, you do not have a "reasonable basis" for expecting to ship within a month.

The shipping date, when provided in your offer, must be clearly and conspicuously stated:

★ ADVERTISEMENT ★
Cardigan Sweaters
S, M, L—Beige or Blue
$29.95 plus tax
Allow 5 weeks for shipment.

If you do not provide a shipping date, you must ship the merchandise within 30 days of receiving a "properly completed" order. An order is properly completed when you receive payment accompanied by all information you need to fill the order. Payment may be made by cash, money order, check, or credit card, according to your company policy. If a credit card is used for a purchase, the order is properly completed when you charge your customer's account.*

When you cannot ship on time, you must provide your customer with an "option" notice. The notice must provide an option to cancel the order and receive a prompt refund, or to agree to a delay in shipping. And, as with the original date, you must have a reasonable basis for setting that shipping date.

You must also have a reasonable basis for telling your customers that you do not know when you can ship merchandise. In that case, you must provide the specific reasons for the shipping problem. For example, you could state that a fire destroyed the warehouse holding the goods and you are unable to provide a revised shipping date because you do not know how long it will take to replace the merchandise.

---

*In 1992 the FTC voted to amend the Rule to cover telephone orders and to redefine "properly completed order" vis-à-vis credit-card sales to mean "as soon as merchants receive enough information to process them, rather than waiting until customers' accounts actually are charged."

WHEN YOU SHOULD SEND A FIRST NOTICE

If a shipment is delayed, the Rule requires that you give your customers an option:

- to consent to a delay; or
- to cancel the order and receive a prompt refund.

People in the trade often refer to the notice as a "delay" notice. More accurately, it should be called an "option" notice. You violate the Rule if you only provide a notice of delay without also providing an option to cancel the order.

Remember, you must send the notice after you first become aware that there will be a shipping delay. The notice must be sent:

- before the promised shipping date; or
- within 30 days after you receive the order (if no date was provided in your solicitation).

WHAT A FIRST NOTICE MUST SAY

If you provide a revised shipping date of 30 days or less, you must have a reasonable basis for making the change. The notice must inform your customers that non-response is considered consent to a delay of 30 days or less.

If you are unable to provide a revised shipping date, your notice must state that you cannot determine when the merchandise will be shipped. It must also state that the order will be automatically canceled unless:

- you ship the merchandise within 30 days of the original shipping date and you have not received your customer's cancellation before shipment; or
- you receive within 30 days of the original date your customer's consent to the delay.

Your notice must provide this information if the definite revised shipping date is more than 30 days after the original date.

When you are unable to provide a revised shipping

date, you must inform your customers of their continuing right to cancel the order by notifying you prior to actual shipment.

When You *May* Cancel an Order

In some cases you can have an option to cancel an order or to send out another notice. You may make this decision when you are unable to ship merchandise on time or within the delay period to which your customer agreed. But if you decide to cancel the order you must inform your customer of this decision and provide a prompt refund.

Whether you cancel or send another notice, you must inform your customer about it within a reasonable time after you know you cannot ship the merchandise.

When You *Must* Cancel an Order

You must cancel an order and provide a prompt refund:
- when your customer does not agree to a delay and exercises the option to cancel an order before it has been shipped;
- when you notify your customer of your inability to ship the merchandise and of your decision to cancel the order;
- when you are unable to ship merchandise before the revised shipping date and you have not received your customer's consent to a further delay;
- when the delay is indefinite and you have not shipped the merchandise or received your customer's consent to an indefinite delay;
- when the definite revised shipping date in the first option notice is more than 30 days after the original shipping date, and you have not shipped the merchandise, nor received your consent to the delay within 30 days of the original shipping date; or

- when you cannot ship on time and do not notify your customers of their options.

All refunds must be sent to the buyer by first class mail. If the buyer paid by cash, check, or money order, you must refund payment within seven (7) days after the order is canceled. For credit card sales, you must make refunds within one billing cycle after the order is canceled. Under no circumstances are you to substitute credit vouchers or scrip for a refund.

WHY YOU SHOULD KEEP RECORDS

If for some reason your company has problems in shipping on time, your customers may begin to file complaints with you, and with local, state, or federal law enforcement agencies. Because the Federal Trade Commission has enforcement jurisdiction under the Mail Order Rule, many complaints are forwarded to the FTC from other agencies.

When the FTC takes action against a company and alleges that it violated the Rule, the company must have records or other documentary proof that will show the steps it took to comply. Systems and procedures for complying with the Rule are carefully reviewed. Lack of such proof creates a rebuttable presumption that the company failed to comply. This means that the seller must be able to show that it used reasonable systems to comply with the Rule. Consequently, it is in your best interest to establish an accurate, up-to-date recordkeeping system.

WHAT THE RULE DOES NOT COVER

The following mail order sales are exempt from the Rule:
- magazine subscriptions (and similar serial deliveries), except for the first shipment;
- sales of seed and growing plants;
- orders made on a collect-on-delivery basis (C.O.D.);

- transactions covered by the FTC's Negative Option Rule* (such as a book and record clubs);
- mail order photo-finishing.

The FTC Mail Order Rule is the one rule all mail-order operators must abide by. Depending on the specifics of your particular business, there may be a few or a slew of other FTC mandates you'll have to deal with. For example, there are rules regarding the labeling of wool, fur, and textile products; rules about disclosure of energy costs or efficiencies of certain home appliances; and rules regarding the advertising of gold and silver jewelry, watches, and precious gems.

The other "rule" you should know about vis-à-vis the FTC is that in its efforts to look out for consumers it is constantly amending its regulations and instituting new ones. This can be annoying for the mail-order operator, but the object of your annoyance should really be all the schemers who are constantly coming up with ways to dupe the public and thus provoke the FTC to place more and more demands on just and unjust entrepreneurs alike. In light of this, you'll need to keep abreast of what's going on at the FTC during startup and the entirety of your business life. For more information on the FTC and how to keep in touch with it, see Chapter 10, Resources.

Once you've settled on the elements of your offer, the next thing to think about is how to present it and your product to the buying public. And so, we turn to advertising.

---

*Negative-option selling is when merchandise (e.g., the book of the month) is sent unless the consumer sends in his or her rejection slip by a certain date.

F I V E

ADVERTISING

You may have all the "right stuff" for making it as an entrepreneur. You may have a dynamite product that was made for mail order. And to top it off you may also have an offer that's too fantastic, too sweet to resist. But if you don't get a mass of mail-order shoppers to take notice, you'll be out of business before you start.

There are many ways to reach the public, and volumes have been written on the how, when, and where of advertising. But the only sure and honest thing anyone can say about advertising in terms of what works and what doesn't can be summed up in two words: It depends. It depends on the particulars of your product and offer, the amount of money you have to spend on advertising, and the flow of your creative and innovative juices. You should also bear in mind that though some people have hit the mark with their very first ad, in most cases the secret of successful advertising is testing and learning from each trial and error.

THE CLASSIFIED AD

The classified advertisement says a lot in a few words. It is the most widely used form of advertising for mail-order businesses for the simple reason that it's relatively inexpensive. Depending on the publications you choose to advertise in, you could pay anywhere from $1 to $7 per word, with most classified ads running about 20 to 30 words.

You can use classified advertising two ways: either to sell your product, or to get inquiries that will give you an opening to make a fuller sales pitch and, you hope, a final sale. To determine how a classified ad will best serve you, you need only look to your product. The more expensive it is, the less success you're likely to have selling it directly through the ad, because most people are reluctant to send off a significant amount of money (over $20) for something on which they only have two or three sentences of information. There are some products, however, that sell very well through mail order with a price of over $20 (books being one of the major ones). Another thing that will make an item a hard sell is if it is so novel that the average mail-order browser could not even picture it. It is rare that a person will buy something, no matter how inexpensive, with which they are totally unfamiliar, unless they have some visual to go by.

If you choose to sell through a classified ad (and assuming people place orders), your follow-up will consist of the simple matter of shipping the goods. If you use an ad to get inquiries, then your follow-up will be the kind of packet you'd create for a direct-mail campaign (discussed in the next chapter).

If the classified ad is your medium of choice, know that

though it isn't that complicated an affair, it does entail a lot of little tasks. The basics are:

• **Finding the right periodicals.** There are literally thousands of places to advertise, and hundreds that might be right for your product. To narrow the field, you'll first have to study up on the possibilities. One way to do this is to buy scores of periodicals and ask friends, neighbors, and relatives to pass theirs along to you when they're done with them. A more systematic approach is to make a trip to the library and spend some time with one or more of the publications of Standard Rate and Data Service (SRDS). SRDS puts out over forty media and marketing resources that will enlighten you on your advertising options and help you make a more informed decision as to where to advertise. The publications that will be most invaluable to you are *Business Publications Rates & Data,* which lists over 5,000 business, technical, and trade publications in the United States; *Consumer Magazines and Agri-Media Rates & Data,* which lists more than 2,000 consumer magazines; *Newspaper Rates & Data,* with some 1,800 entries; and *Community Publications Rates & Data,* with its 2,300-plus entries. Finding the right periodical in these books won't be like searching through the proverbial haystack, because they are arranged in categories. For example *Consumer Magazines and Agri-Media Rates & Data* is arranged alphabetically in seventy editorial classifications, such as "Art and Antiques," "Brides and Bridal," "Mystery, Adventure, and Science Fiction," "Sports," "Travel," "Women's Fashion," and "Youth." In addition to informing you about what publications are out there, these SRDS books include an editorial profile of a publication, its ad rates (the cost), its basic mechanical requirements (what you have to submit and how you have to submit it), and its closing date (the date you'd need to get your ad in for such-and-such issue). The SRDS publications aren't cheap, so it's advisable to check them out first at a library. Should you want to consider buying them, or if you simply want a little more information about SRDS's entire line of books, write for a product catalogue: Standard Rate & Data Service, 3004 Glenview Road, Wilmette, IL 60091.

Once you've identified the publications most appropriate for your product—that is, those geared toward people most likely to be interested in what you're selling—the next item on your agenda is to get acquainted with these publications. The cheapest way to do this is to camp out at the library and read several issues of each publication under consideration. If this is inconvenient or virtually impossible, then you'll have to pick up current issues at your newsstand and order back issues from the publisher.

In studying the publications, what you're looking for is those that will give you the most for your money. As a rule, it means those with the largest circulation (the larger the readership, the greater the chance of multitudes seeing your ad) and the healthiest mail-order advertising section (if a lot of other mail-order companies advertise in a publication, it must be for a pretty good reason; namely, that it gets them results). It also means advertising in magazines over newspapers for the simple reason that people tend to dispose of newspapers as soon as they are done with them, whereas magazines hang around and are passed along. Obviously, the longer a periodical "lives," the greater the number of people who will read or at least flip through it and thus the greater the number of people who will see your ad. These criteria only hold true if you're dealing in a general-interest product—an item that appeals to men or women (or both) regardless of their race, color, creed, or favorite pastime.

After you've made your first cut of publications, call or write the semi-finalists—Attention: Classified Advertising Manager—requesting an ad kit that will spell out everything you need to know and do to place an ad. This may be unnecessary for some of the publications you come across, because all the information is included within the pages of each issue.

• **Timing.** The issue in which you run an ad may matter a lot or a little. If you're dealing in something seasonal, then obviously you should run it during the months people are most likely to be shopping for such items. If you're carrying a product that's for all seasons, your only concern is to have your ad in one of the publication's strongest issues. Although this varies from publication to publication, take note that experts have found that ads for mail-order products tend to pull best in January, February, October, and November, with the summer months pulling worst. This is just a guide. The way to determine which months are best for your product is to run an ad in different issues of the same publication. According to conventional wisdom, you will receive about 50 percent of your responses within four to five weeks from the date the ad ran. So if you receive 200 orders a month after your ad ran, you can safely assume that an ad's total draw will be about 400 orders. As to when you'll get your total, only time will tell. It could take three months, four months, or even a year.

• **Creating the copy.** You don't have to be a professional writer to write effective ad copy, just observant. If you study what others have done, you'll soon get the hang of it. Below are some examples of classified ads taken from various publications (thus the omission of contact numbers/addresses).

BE YOUR OWN BOSS! 1001 fast, easy ways to make money! Free! Rush name, address.

JANITORIAL BUSINESS MONEYMAKING SECRETS—Make $40,000+ annually starting from scratch. FREE BUSINESS REPORT!

HUGE PROFIT POTENTIAL with your 900 number. Send $14.95 for guidebook to:

THE RIGHT AD MAKES MONEY. No nonsense, successful advertising techniques. Rush $9.95 to:

CREATE A SUCCESSFUL PRESS RELEASE. Special report! Send $7.50:

HOME IMPORT MAIL-ORDER business. Start without capital. Free report.

2,000 QUALITY IMPORTS: BRASSWARE, household porcelain. Catalog $3.00

LEARN INTERIOR DECORATING. Home study. Free literature.

MONEY IN MAIL ORDER? ABSOLUTELY! Let our powerful handbooks show you how. Free brochure.

As you can see, a classified ad isn't short and sweet, but short and aggressive, short and punchy, short and to-the-point. It projects a sense of urgency—or as others have put it, a classified ad is a call to action. In order to move people to act, you must keep focused on the only two things shoppers need to know: the WHAT and the HOW.

The WHAT is your product or more information on it. Here are ten tips on getting people to take notice of it and heed your call to action

1. *Use an attention-getting headline.* Lead with what is special or unique about your product (e.g., "Rare coins"; "One-of-a-kind teapots"), or what it will do for the consumer (e.g., "Save money," "End clutter," "Get slim fast"), or with an incentive (the best passwords here are "Free" and "No risk").

2. *Use phrases.* No complete sentences. Talk shorthand. Remember, words are money. Also, people don't want to spend a lot of time reading.

3. *Use words that appeal to the senses, the emotions.* Appeal to the heart, the gut, not the intellect.

4. *Use simple language.* Avoid hundred-dollar words, or language that could confuse and hence lose the browser.

5. *Be blunt.* Avoid euphemisms or fuzzy language. Use "Free" instead of "At no charge" and "Limited supply" (if such is the case) as opposed to "Offer available while supplies last."

6. *Use dynamic punctuation.* Don't stop with the period. Enliven your ad with exclamation marks, question marks, and dashes.

7. *Use* UPPERCASING *or* **boldfacing** *or italics* as affordable and as available so that key words or phrases stand out. (Some publications don't offer boldfacing; many offer the first three or four words uppercased for free.)

8. *Use figures instead of words for numbers.* This will save you money because most numbers spell out to two or more words ($1 versus one dollar). It will also save the reader time, because we process figures more quickly than we do words. "Over 50 kinds of puzzles" is a faster read than "Over fifty kinds of puzzles."

9. *Use symbols as substitutes for words.* As with numbers, familiar symbols such as "&," "#," "=," and "$" are processed more quickly than words.
10. *Use abbreviations.* This, too, speeds up the reading. But be sure to use standard and common abbreviations.

Presenting the WHAT is admittedly the hardest part. Giving people the lowdown on the HOW—what they must do to get the WHAT—is easier. Still, it takes thought. Here are five pointers.

1. A lot of people find a SASE (self-addressed, stamped envelope) a hassle. If you saw two ads for a brochure on a line of, say, candles, and one asked for a SASE and the other didn't, to which would you respond? If you are going to request a SASE, know that most people will send a #10 envelope (business size) and some the smaller #6, with postage for a one-ounce first-class letter. So if what you'll be sending requires a larger envelope and/or more postage, you should specify the size of the envelope and amount of postage people need to send. For example: "Send 52¢ in stamps" or "Send 10x13 envelope." Of course such requirements may turn a lot of people off. So if you cannot afford to foot the bill for mailing out your information, an alternative is to ask for, say, $1 "for postage and handling."
2. People are more like to respond to an offer for information if it is free. The less something costs, the more apt we are to give in to our curiosity. However, most people do understand that they can't always get something for nothing. If you must charge for your information, it shouldn't be more than a few dollars. The price should be rounded to the nearest dollar, because since people are most likely to send cash, they don't want to be bothered with wrapping coins. So don't ask for $2.50, but either $2 or $3.

3. Unless you're limiting the method of payment to one, don't waste space with instructions like "Send cash, check or money order for $12." "Send $12" will do. Given no specific directive, people will send payment by the method that is most convenient for them.

4. If your ad is for your product and you do not anticipate having a problem delivering the goods within 30 days of receipt of the order, then there's no need to specify a delivery date. If it could take longer, then you'd better note that in your ad. Remember, if you don't and there's a shipping delay, the FTC may get you for violating the Rule.

5. Dispense with Street, Avenue, etc. in your address unless doing so could result in misdelivered mail. If your address is "789 Sunkist Street" and there's no Sunkist Avenue or Boulevard in your area, "789 Sunkist" will suffice.

• **Keying the ad.** "Keying" is putting a code in the ad that will enable you to tell which ads brought in what orders. The key consists of a series of letters, numbers, or both that identify the name and issue of the publication. In inquiry ads, the code is sometimes in the title of the information to be requested. For example, if you were running an ad offering a brochure of your Easy Chore line of products in *Lazy Living, Armchair Traveler*, and *Modern Couch Potato* magazines, you might assign the magazines the numbers 1, 2, and 3 respectively, and in the ads instruct readers to "Request Catalog #1" and so forth. If you were running the ads in the January and March issues of the magazines and wanted to see which months pulled better, then your instructions would read, "Request Catalog #1-1" (for January) and "Request Catalog #1-3" (for March) and so forth.

This method of keying may fail you, because it only works if the inquiring minds follow instructions. In many cases a customer may simply write for "your catalogue of

Easy Chore products" and you won't know which magazine pulled that request. The best place to put your key is in the address, because people are more attentive to details when addressing an envelope. You do this by using "Dept." or "Suite" followed by the initials of the publication and a number for the month or issue number. Using the above scenario, your contact information might read: "789 Sunkist, Dept. LL1."

As you can see, although a classified is a little bitty thing, it takes a lot of thought to get it right. By way of review, let's take a look at a before-and-after example of the writing of one.

BEFORE: We have a very large selection of handmade silk scarves with motifs and signature imagery of various cultures from around the world, including the Middle East, Africa, Asia, and Latin America. If you would like a copy of our current catalog, please send three dollars to: Exotica Enterprises, 123 West Moonbeam Street, Woowee, NY 45678. When you write, we'd appreciate it if you'd mention that you saw this ad in *Taste of Beauty* magazine.

AFTER: HUGE SELECTION of handmade silk scarves with ethnic designs—Middle Eastern, African, Asian, Latin American and more! Catalog $3. Exotica, 123 W. Moonbeam, Dept. TOB, Woowee, NY 45678.

THE DISPLAY AD

Because a display advertisement—anywhere from a few inches to a full page—is larger than a classified ad, it gets your product noticed more. The larger the ad, the stronger the pitch you can make. As with a classified ad, you can use a display ad to solicit either orders or inquiries. But since a display ad is many times more expensive than a classified ad (costing anywhere from a several hundred dollars to several thousand), you'll make the most of your money if you use it for direct selling.

Most display ads contain some kind of illustration. This visual representation of your product could be a photograph or a drawing. The choice is yours and should be based on what will best show off your wares. In some instances an illustration might be best because it can convey a certain spirit or mood.

In the copy, you would use the same basic techniques you would use for a classified ad, only you would stretch the story of your product and offer out a little. Also, your prose might be a bit less clipped.

The other matter of concern is the layout: how the illustration and the copy are positioned within the space. Generally the visual matter is on top, followed by the copy and ordering information, which might include a coupon. In many ads the illustration takes up 50 percent of the space, and in other cases a lot less or a lot more. The ratio of art and words should be based on what your product demands. If people need to see something to get your product, then let illustration take priority. If there are a lot of things people need to know about your product or your offer, then let text reign. As for the look of the ad, you could go busy or airy, depending on the image you wish to project or the attitude you want to convey.

A display ad is clearly more effective by virtue of the fact that it's more eye-catching than a classified ad. And as a rule, the bigger the ad, the more eyes it will catch. But keeping eyes trained on the ad long enough to get readers not merely to react but to act is contingent upon the strength of your product and the composition of the ad. So don't make the mistake of thinking that there's something magical about the display ad in and of itself. Like the classified ad, it's only a doorbell, albeit one that rings a little louder. As powerful as a display ad might be, however, it's inadvisable to make it your first mode of advertising unless you know what you're doing. If you have never placed an ad in your life and don't know a layout from a lay-up, you should start with a classified ad. It's cheaper and simpler and thus a good place to get your feet wet in the world of print advertising. By the same token, print advertising is the place to start when it comes to the world of advertising in general. For while radio, network and cable television are very viable modes of marketing mail-order wares— especially if you feature a toll-free number—you shouldn't consider broadcast media unless you have beaucoup bucks to spare. If you are curious about the cost of audio and visual advertising, take note that Standard Rate and Data Service's line of publications includes *Spot Television Rates and Data* and *Spot Radio Rates and Data*.

"FREE" ADVERTISING

The smaller your advertising budget, the more creative you'll have to be. One of the popular strategies is a press release. (This might better be termed "cheap" advertising, since it will cost you something to produce and distribute.) A press release is usually a one- or two-pager on what you're doing, rendered in such a way as to make it seem newsworthy. It would be sent to various media in hopes that some editor will want to do a story on your product or your business in general, or at least include you in one already on the drawing board. The idea is that getting some press will get you some business. Some people swear by this, others consider it a total waste of paper and postage. As with the other modes of advertising, you won't know if it'll work for you unless you try it. Clearly, if you send a press release about your line of stainless-steel tweezers to an editor at a major national publication, chances are it'll end up in the trash before it's halfway read. But if there's something novel about your product or there's something noteworthy or extraordinary about your being an entrepreneur, there's a greater chance of your ending up in the news—greater still with a community or local media organ. The point: Aim high but be realistic. And if you are going to try the press release, don't limit yourself to the media. Consider the newsletters or bulletins of your alumni association or other professional, social, or religious organizations of which you are a member. Depending on how copy-needy the organ is for a particular issue, its policy on unsolicited stories, and how well they know you (or like you), you may have the entire release reprinted or it may be edited down into a short announcement.

No matter who gets your press release, remember, it won't be a worthwhile shot if you don't tell your story in such a way as to make others sit up and take notice.

As you go to the drawing board on your paid or "free" advertising plans, keep the following in mind.

1. **Don't be too proud or cheap to get help.** Sure, the more of a do-it-yourselfer you are, the better. But if there are aspects of advertising—writing, drawing, layout—that are simply not your thing and never will be, get help. If you can't find it among your network of friends and associates, then you can shop for that writer, graphic artist, or advertising consultant in the classified-ad sections of small business and mail-order-interest publications.

2. **Follow the leader.** If you can handle the technicals but are weak in the concept department, read around and model your ad on what seems to be working for others. Similarly, when trying to figure out what publications and type of ad is best for you, take note of what others who are selling the same or similar product(s) are doing, and do likewise.

3. **Get critiqued.** Before you place an ad, share it with people whose opinions and instincts you trust. The

more specific you are about what you want by way of feedback, the better they'll serve you. So don't just say, "What do you think?" Rather, put specific questions to them, such as "Is it easy to read?" "Does it make sense?" "Is it too aggressive?" "Does it in anyway insult the reader?" "Is it too busy?"

SIX

DIRECT-MAIL CAMPAIGN

Many mail-order operators don't go for print advertising. Instead they prefer to cut to the chase. That is, they get the information on their merchandise into the mailboxes of people most likely to be interested in it by waging a direct-mail campaign.

THE PACKET

The basic components of a direct-mail packet are:

• **The Outer Envelope.** This may be a plain envelope with nothing on it except your return address and the recipient's. Or it may have a short sales pitch or other come-on, such as "Personal and Confidential," "You may have already won . . . ," "Urgent," or "Open Immediately." The disadvantage of a come-on is that it's trite. More than anything else, it advertises that the contents are unsolicited mail. In general, people who open mail with "come-ons" will open anything—including a plain envelope. Another tactic is to have little handwritten notes on the front or back of the envelope. Something chatty, such as "Mary, hope to hear from you soon." The idea is to make the recipients think they are hearing from someone they know. There are two problems with this. One, it's time-consuming. Two, it can backfire, since a lot of people will resent you for duping them into opening your mail and will decide immediately not to hear you out.

Many mail-order experts advocate the plain approach on the theory that the less of an idea a person has of what's inside the envelope, the more curious they'll be and thus the more apt to open it. If you choose to go plain, take care not go too low-budget. A chintzy envelope with a rubber-stamped return address and a crooked mailing label is a dead giveaway that it's unsolicited mail that few but the lonely or very bored will open. Also, people will consciously or subconsciously read it as indicative of the quality of your merchandise.

• **The Sales Letter.** This is the heart and soul of your direct-mail packet. It's the equivalent of a face-to-face sales pitch. Here are some tips on style and substance:

The Tone. Keep it conversational but not too chatty. Keep it brisk but not cold.

The Opening. Like the headline for a classified ad, your opening sentence must be an attention getter. You might intrigue your reader with a question such as "Would you like to put an end to clutter?" or "Did you know that . . . ?" Or your opening might be a claim or significant fact about your product. Whatever it is, it should arise organically from the product. Also, it should not insult the reader.

The Body. Here's where you describe what you're selling and what it'll do for the reader (or someone the reader knows and loves). You might also include information about yourself or your company—but only if you have an interesting story to tell. Any additional information you provide should enhance your product's appeal, not distract people from it. After you've given folks the scoop on your product, you then move on to talk about the specifics of your offer.

The Closure. Your objective here is to persuade your reader to act and act now! You don't accomplish this by repeating yourself, but rather with some aggressive but polite directive, such as "Call our toll-free number today!" or "Send in your order today! Don't delay!," and any "news" of the bonus for an immediate response, if such is in your plans.

The Postscript. Many marketing professionals recommend adding a P.S. to your letter, because research has shown that because a P.S. is eye-catching and suggestive of some secret or extra-special message, people really do read them, and if the letter is a one-pager, very often people read the P.S. first. Your P.S. might be the restatement of a key point you made about your product or a reiteration of the urgency of ordering ASAP.

The Look. Use the standard format for a business letter and reader-friendly print. You might want to jazz up the letter with some graphics, but if you do, take care not to make it too busy. The look of the letter should be consistent with the image you want to project. When in doubt, keep it simple and traditional. And don't forget to triple-check it for typographical and grammatical errors. Before you put it into production, have someone "fluent" in standard American English proofread it.

The Form of Address. You wouldn't dream of writing "Hey, you!" would you? Then remember that "Dear Occupant" or "Dear Reader" is equally off-putting. Although it means a smidgen more work, you should personalize the letter. The safest way to go is "Dear Ms. Anderson." "Dear Dorothy" is presumptuous, and "Dear Dorothy Anderson" is a bit too stiff.

The Length. A sales letter can be one page or several pages long. Your product and offer should determine the length. Although people like to get through their mail quickly, don't keep it short on principle.

• **Supporting Materials.** This might be a flyer with a photograph or drawing of your product or its components. The image may be of the product alone or of someone using or enjoying it—any kind of visual that will help you clinch a sale, because visuals do speak volumes. If you have a product that comes in assorted colors, finishes, or textures, you might affix a color chart or swatches to the page. If you're selling more than one product, then a brochure or mini-catalogue with a description and perhaps an image of each item will be in order.

Another kind of supporting material is the testimonial. Many people recommend including one or more testimonials in your packet for the simple reason that a satisfied consumer is your best salesperson. Testimonials are acquired one of two ways. If you've sold your product through an ad, door to door, or in some other forum, you may already have received some unsolicited praise from a happy customer or two. If you haven't, you could contact previous customers and ask them to comment on the goods. If your direct-mail campaign is your first outreach action, then you could send samples to a select number of people and ask them to react to your wares in writing. Whether you use solicited or unsolicited rave reviews, full-blown testimonials or just a quoteworthy word or two, you will need to have the testimonial givers sign a release giving you permission to use all or part of their comments for advertising purposes. And to handle this properly, you should consult an attorney. If a testimonial sounds like more work than you've time for, don't sweat it. Many consumers are skeptical about testimonials, and including them in your packet may have either no impact or a negative impact on the recipient.

• **The Guarantee.** Even if you mention your guarantee in the sales letter, it's a good idea to present it as a separate document. As already discussed, a money-back guarantee inspires confidence. A guarantee in the form of a certificate is a strong reminder that you aim to please.

• **The Order Blank.** This is a must because it makes ordering simple for the consumer and order processing easier for you. Your order form should have all the boxes, lines, and columns needed to remind the consumer to provide all the information you will need to fill the order. The most needful things are the customer's name, address, and daytime phone number, and product information such as quantity, item number, description, color, and size as applicable. Other features of a comprehensive order form are spaces for method of payment if you're allowing more than one option and other money matters such as unit price, extended price, merchandise total, sales tax (if applicable), shipping and handling charges, and the sum total. With shipping and handling charges, if you are charging a flat fee regardless of the size of the order, then you should have that charge on the form; if not, you should provide a scale or rate chart. Where you put your order form will depend on the components of your direct-mail packet. For example, it may be at the bottom of your flyer, inside your brochure (stapled or loose), or behind your sales letter.

• **The Self-Addressed Envelope.** Yes, this is another expense, but since it facilitates ordering for the consumer, it's worth it. The issue you'll need to think about for more than a minute is whether or not to pay for the postage.

Doing so will make ordering that much easier for your customers, but it'll mean another expense for you. Should you decide to pay the postage, the best way to do so is to get a permit (from the post office) for the business-reply-mail imprint. If you use SASEs you'll lose money every time someone doesn't order, whereas with postage-paid envelopes you only pay for those envelopes returned to you.

There are hundreds of varieties of direct-mail packets— from the very modest to the very slick. If you want to get a gander at what others are doing, turn to your mailbox (and those of your friends and family members). Study the campaigns others are waging. See what turns you off and what turns you on. Most important, think about what will appeal to your particular market. When you find a campaign on which you'd like to model yours, take it to a printer or two for an estimate on how much it would cost (per thousand, per two thousand, and so on) and then scale yours up or down based on your findings and your budget.

THE POSTAGE

Production is the major cost concern when it comes to developing and designing your direct-mail packet, but postage is no small matter. The more the packet weighs, the more it'll cost to mail. Postage isn't cheap and is forever going up. When you're mailing a single piece, an ounce more or less is very small change. But when that small change is multiplied by thousands, you're talking big bucks. For example, let's say your direct-mail packet weighs 4 ounces and you're mailing out 5,000. Your postage (at 1993 rates) would be 98 cents per piece (for 5 ounces and under, there's no difference between first-class and third-class), or $4,900. If, by using a lighter-weight paper, by making the packet a self-mailer, or through some other kind of redesigning you were able to bring the piece down to 3 ounces, you'd then be paying 75 cents per piece, or $3,750—for a savings of $1,150. You could further reduce your expense for postage by opting out of first class and into either third-class bulk or presort first-class mail, both of which are only for sending out multiples of identical matter. For third-class bulk, the per-piece weight must be less than 16 ounces and the mailing minimum is 200 pieces or 50 pounds. For presort first class, the per-piece weight must be less than 11 ounces and the mailing minimum is 500 pieces. With third-class bulk you can save 10 cents or more per piece, and with presort first class, about 4 cents. You pay for the money you save on postage with your labor: you have to prepare the mail according to certain sorting, labeling, and bundling specifications. This is a rather tedious and time-consuming affair; but the good news is that the post office holds seminars on the procedures and supplies you with the stickers, rubber bands, and sacks necessary for preparing the mailing properly. You should also know that there's an annual fee (about $75) for both of these services, as well as a one-time fee for the permit to imprint the "Bulk Rate" or "Presort First-Class" box on your envelope or the address side of a self-mailer. Between the work you have to do and the fees, third-class bulk or presort first class only makes sense if you'll be doing large mailings on some kind of regular basis.

THE MAILING LIST

To get a mailing list, you can do one or a combination of a few things. One strategy is to solicit inquiries through an ad and thereby start developing what's known as your House List. Another is to compile your own list from your Rolodex (and those of your friends and relatives), public records, college and university alumni directories, directories of organizations and associations, and even the telephone directories if you want to reach out and touch business.

Developing a mailing list yourself can be a very time-consuming and exhausting, especially if you aren't an experienced or natural-born researcher. A third and less taxing strategy is to deal with a list broker. List brokers rent lists they have themselves compiled and/or function as intermediaries between people in search of mailing lists and businesses and institutions that rent their customer or membership lists. With a list broker you'll be able to find lists of people who fit all kinds of categories. For example, people who engage in a particular hobby; people who are known mail-order buyers; people who have purchased a particular product of category of goods; people who are in a particular line of work, trade, or profession, people who fit a specific profile for example, urban marrieds with children and a pet and an annual income of $50,000 to $75,000.

Mailing lists rent for as little as $35 and as much as $100 per thousand (with 5,000 being the minimum for most firms). List brokers will not only help you find the right list(s), they will also help you expedite your mailing by supplying the names on labels or floppy disks or affixing labels to envelopes you supply. But be wary: More than a few direct-mail campaigns have failed because while the packet was sublime, the mailing list was a disaster—full of names of dead people, nonexistent people, and folks who have long since moved from the address you were given. Suffice it to say, it's imperative to deal with a reputable, established list broker. To find one, check your telephone directory or the classified advertising section of mail-order and general small-business periodicals. Then write or call a few of them for complete information on their service.

One way to get the lay of the mailing list land (and perhaps do without a list broker) is to take a trip to the library and look up the SRDS publication *Direct Mail Lists Rates and Data*. It is a compilation of over 10,000 mailing lists on the rental market, with descriptions of the lists and other information, including rental rates and restrictions on usage. This publication also contains profiles of list brokers and consultants.

When shopping for mailing lists, bear in mind that though price is not always an indicator of quality, there's something to the adage that you get what you pay for.

If you opt for waging a direct-mail campaign instead of or in addition to print advertising, remember the three simple rules discussed at the end of the last chapter.

1. **Don't be too proud or cheap to get help.**
2. **Follow the leader.**
3. **Get critiqued.**

SEVEN

THE WRAP

When orders arrive in your mailbox, it'll be time to rejoice—and get busy on the simplest albeit most labor-intensive aspect of a mail-order business: fulfillment, otherwise known as processing the orders and delivering the goods.

The first good habit you need to get into is opening your mail without delay. When you remove an order from the envelope you should post on it the date of receipt, preferably with a date stamp. Then scrutinize the order to make sure you have everything you need to fill the order. If a customer has sent insufficient information or funds, you should contact him or her immediately for clarity or the balance due.

The next optional step is to acknowledge receipt of the order. You can do this with a form letter or postcard in which you first thank customers for their orders received on such-and-such a date and then advise them that their merchandise will arrive on or before such-and-such a date. This is purely a courtesy, a building block for good customer relations.

The next step is, of course, to get the merchandise out. You should do this ASAP. Ideally, the day the order is received—except in cases where payment was a check, in which case you should wait until the check clears. Also, unless your mail-order business is the only thing on your plate, it may be impossible to get orders out ASAP. If this is the case, you should designate one day of the week or certain chunks of time during the week for picking and packing orders and getting them into the mail or hands of UPS or another carrier.

One of the absolute musts of a operating a mail-order business is keeping a record of the history of every order (incoming and outgoing). This will enable you to follow up on any shipping foul-ups and keep track of how your business is doing. Whether you record the information upon shipping out the merchandise or in stages (part upon receipt of the order, part upon shipping) is a matter of choice. All that matters is that you do it.

The most important data is the customer information (name, address, telephone), merchandise information (quantity, size, color, style, as applicable), and the dates an order was received and shipped. To see the entire story of an order at a glance, you need to create a form with space to record other data, including payment information (the amount and method of payment) and your shipping cost. If you sold your product through an ad, you'll need a space for the key code so you'll know how the different ads are performing. The more data there is to record, the more ingenious you'll need to be when it comes to designing a workable form.

To get an idea of the possibilities, take a look at the following forms for the widget seller we met earlier. For the

Date rec'd	Customer name	Customer address	Qty.	$ Sent	M.O.P.	Date filled	Source	Postage
3/1/93	Mary Smith	123 Main Street #4 Anywhere, USA 98765 (222) 333-4444	5	$100	Check	3/15/93	LL3*	$5.67

*The key for an ad placed in the March issue of *Lazy Living* magazine.

Customer: (Name) _____

(Address) _____

_____

(Phone) _____

Date rec'd: _____

Amt. rec'd: _____

M.O.P.: _____

DMP:* _____

DMP#:† _____

Item #1: _____ Description: _____ Qty.: _____ Date shipped: _____ Carrier: _____ Postage: _____

Item #2: _____ Description: _____ Qty.: _____ Date shipped: _____ Carrier: _____ Postage: _____

Item #3: _____ Description: _____ Qty.: _____ Date shipped: _____ Carrier: _____ Postage: _____

Item #4: _____ Description: _____ Qty.: _____ Date shipped: _____ Carrier: _____ Postage: _____

Comments:‡ _____

_____

_____

_____

_____

*For the date the direct-mail packet was sent out.

†If he had sent out a couple of different versions of his direct-mail packet and keyed them as DMP #1, DMP #2, and so on.

‡For recording information from any written or oral contact with a customer.

68

first one, the scenario is as follows: he sells nothing but widgets, and only one kind; he sells through a classified ad in several magazines; he ships all orders via USPS. The second one is for orders garnered through a direct-mail campaign. And in this instance Mr. X carries widgets in a rainbow of colors and various widget accessories. Also, in addition to USPS, he ships via UPS and Federal Express.

The wisdom of record keeping will become more apparent as your mail-order days wear on, for as your initial orders come in and the merchandise goes out, the data will be vital in problem solving on many fronts. The areas of primary concern are most likely to be complaints, inventory, and your advertising encore.

You should commit yourself to handling complaints with the same speed and care you give to depositing the payments and filling the orders. You will avoid a lot of frustration if you hold fast to the doctrine of old that the customer is always right.

As for inventory, you should adjust the amount you keep on hand based on the rate of arrival and size of your first wave of orders and the amount of money you can afford to have tied up in stock. Even if your starting inventory flew out, if you can get restocked within a day or two there's no need to carry a large inventory. But it takes 30, 60, or more days for you to get the goods, then it may be in your best interest to reorder big. There's nothing worse than having a stack of prepaid orders and no goods—except, of course, having oodles of stock without a single order. In short, inventory management is as much a matter of common sense as it is of instincts. That is why you must first analyze your order records for any flukes or patterns and then go with your gut. Simply knowing how much merchandise moved isn't enough.

For example, if you stocked 1,000 ceramic mugs and shipped out half your stock within two weeks of your ad's hitting, you might be inclined to reorder at least another 500, and you might be moved to gamble on another 1,000.

But if after reviewing your records you remembered that one customer had ordered 200 mugs, you'd know to place a more cautious reorder. Selling x amount of goods to 10 people is not as good an indicator as selling the same amount of goods to 100 people. Inventory will become more manageable with time, for it is only with the passage of time that you'll get a feel for your product's selling season and the peak and valley points within that time.

When it comes to your advertising or direct-mail encore, remember: if it ain't broke, don't fix it. That is, if your ads pulled very well, don't change a thing, just keep running them. Of course, to be more precise about it, you should review your records to determine which ads pulled what percentage of orders. Should you find that one ad only brought in a small number of orders, then you should drop out of that publication and try another. If your direct-mail packet brought in big business, don't tamper with success, just rent or compile another batch of names and do another mailing.

But what if your first response wasn't so hot? Well, you don't collapse and crumble into a corner. You try, try, and try again. Finding the problem could be tricky. For one, it could be your price. The only way to tell would be to rerun your original ads or resend your direct-mail piece (with appropriate revisions), offering your wares at a reduced price. The problem could be in your ad copy or the direct-mail piece itself. The only way to determine this would be to recraft it and rerun or resend it. Another possibility is that you missed your market. In the case of print advertising, this would mean that you made a poor choice of publications. In the case of a direct-mail campaign, you may have compiled or rented a terrible list, in which case you should either swallow your pride and deal with a list broker or talk with the firm you used to see if they can offer any explanation of why their list failed to perform.

The final and most painful possibility is that there was

nothing wrong with your price, your advertising venue, or the medium, but rather, nobody wanted what you were selling. This isn't really ascertainable, however, until you've tried, tried, and tried again. You should keep this prescription for handling a first failure uppermost in your mind when planning your enterprise. And before you say yes to getting into the mail-order business, you must consider this: If you can't afford—emotionally or financially—to fail your first time out, you can't afford to get into the mail-order business.

EIGHT

ON BUSINESS AFFAIRS

L ong, *long* gone are the days when you could just up and sell your wares at will, at whim, and without answering to anyone. Granted, a lot of folks do operate this way today, but then, a lot of folks are constantly looking over their shoulders.

As is the case with any business, your mail-order business will be a lot of people's business. These "people" are various government agencies who exist to keep you in check and keep track of what you're up to, as well as to help you protect your interests. So if you want to start smart, you'll have to be able to weave your way through a fair amount of bureaucracy, which will generally translate into a battery of telephone calls and a pile of paperwork. You'll also need a good understanding of conduct becoming a proper mail-order operator.

PERMITS, LICENSES, ETC.

• **Zoning.** Local ordinances on the kinds of business that can be operated within a certain area and from a residence vary from community to community, with regulations being less restrictive in mixed-use zones (residential and commercial) than in residential zones. In all likelihood, zoning laws will be the least of your problems. As a rule, if your business won't be problematic for your neighbors, landlord, or co-op board, you probably won't have any problems with the zoning czar. Also, because most zoning laws are decades old, and consequently out of step with our modern lives and times, variances are often granted in cases when a business is technically prohibited. But you shouldn't assume anything. Get the facts. To do so, go to your own town or city hall and read up on the regulations, or call and ask what office handles zoning and then contact it.

• **Business Licenses.** Depending on the specifics of your business and where you live, your local government may require you to get a license or permit. Getting one will entail little more than filing an application and paying a small fee. To find out if you will need one and, if so, information on the application process, contact your local business licensing board. If such is not listed in your local telephone directory, you can find out what agency handles business licenses at your city or town hall or county clerk's office. To find out if you will need a state license, contact your state's state department or your state's state information center (see Chapter 10, Resources, for details).

• **Import/Export.** You don't need a license to import merchandise, but since importing goods can involve a lot of red tape and expense, you should familiarize yourself with the rules, regulations, and procedures for importing before you decide to deal in goods that aren't made in

America. Should you decide to make your mail-order business international, you may need an export license, depending on what your product is and where you'll be selling it. For information on matters of import and export, contact Customs (part of the Treasury Department) and the Department of Commerce.

• **Fictitious Name Statement.** This is also known as an Assumed Named Certificate or a DBA (doing business as). It will be necessary if you plan to do business as a sole proprietor (discussed later in this chapter) under a name other than your own. When it comes to choosing a name for your business, keep it short and simple. The easiest pick is your first and last name, or last name only plus "Associates," "Group," or "Company" (unless you're incorporated you can't use "Inc."). The other logical choice for a business name is one that is descriptive or in some way indicative of the nature of your business, such as Widgets and Things. Words like "& Things" or "Etc." allow you to expand your product-line selection without having to change the name of your company to avoid confusing the public about what you carry. The only problem with using a name than doesn't include your name is that to avoid a possible lawsuit you have to conduct a search to make sure that your proposed name isn't already in use in your area, either by another sole proprietor, an in-state company, or an out-of-state company that may have exclusive rights to a name because they do business in your state. You can have an attorney do a search for you or you can do it yourself. If you choose to handle it yourself, be advised that you'll have to go through many checkpoints if you want to be thorough. These include your county's fictitious name registry, your secretary of state's listing of businesses based and doing business in your state, and the Federal Trademark Registry.

Once you've decided on a name that's sensible and safe to use, the process of registering is relatively simple. It involves getting a business certificate form (available at your county clerk's office and any stationer that carries legal forms), filling it out in triplicate, having it notarized, filing it with your county clerk, and getting certified copies (two being the recommended number). After you've filed the statement, you'll be required to publish the information in a local newspaper as a way of putting the public on notice that you are doing business under such-and-such a name. For complete information on the process, contact your county clerk.

• **Seller's Permit.** This is also known as a resale certificate or resale number. What it "permits" you to do is purchase your inventory or the raw materials for your product from wholesalers and retailers without paying sales tax. What it obligates you to do is remit to the government (on a monthly or quarterly basis) the sales tax you collect from consumers on the product. For complete information on a seller's permit, contact your state sales-and-use-tax department. Depending on where you live, it may be under the auspices of the Department of Revenue, the Department of Taxation, the State Tax Commission, or the State Tax Department. When you make your inquiry, you can find out other information, such as the schedule for sales tax remittance, whether you have to charge tax on out-of-state sales, and whether you are to charge tax on merchandise only or on the merchandise and shipping charge.

• **Legal Organization.** Every business has to have an identity. The options are sole proprietorship, partnership, or corporation. The following description of the first two options is taken from the IRS publication *Tax Guide for Small Businesses.*

Sole Proprietorships. A sold proprietor is the simplest form of business organization. The business has no existence apart from you, the owner. Its liabilities are your personal liabilities, and your proprietary interests end when you die. You undertake the risks of business to the extent of all assets, whether used in the business or personally owned.

Profit or loss. When you figure your taxable income for the year, you must add in any profit, or subtract out any loss, you have from your sole proprietorship. You must report the profit or loss from each of your businesses operated as a sole proprietorship on a separate Schedule C (Form 1040), *Profit or Loss from Business.* The amount of this business profit or loss is entered as an item of profit or loss on your individual income tax return Form 1040.

If you are a sole proprietor, you are probably liable for **self-employment tax.** . . . You ordinarily will have to make estimated tax payments.*

Partnerships. A partnership is not a taxable entity. However, it must figure its profit or loss and file a return. A partnership files its return on Form 1065, *U.S. Partnership Return of Income*

A partnership is the relationship existing between two or more persons who join together to carry on a trade or business. Each person contributes money, property, labor, or skill and expects to share in the profits and losses of the business.

For income tax purposes, the term partnership includes a syndicate group, pool, joint venture, or other unincorporated organization that is carrying on a business and that is not classified as a trust, estate, or corporation.

A joint undertaking to share expenses is **not** a partnership. Mere coownership of property that is main-

---

*This tax is levied against your net business income (gross minus all allowable deductions) and goes into our national social security and medicare "pots." The self-employment tax (about 15%) is in addition to any federal, state, or local income taxes.

tained or leased or rented is **not** a partnership. However, if the co-owners provide services to the tenants, a partnership exists.

Partnership agreement. The partnership agreement includes the original agreement and any modifications of it agreed to by all the partners or adopted in any other manner provided by the partnership agreement. The agreement or modifications may be oral or written.

As you can see, with these two forms of business you or you and your partner are the business, and "making it so" is done when you file your taxes. The downside, however, is that because you and your business are one and the same, if your business should be sued, your personal assets are in jeopardy. The disadvantage peculiar to partnerships is that one partner is liable for the actions of the other(s) taken on behalf of the business. This liability can be minimized, however, by entering into what is known as a limited partnership versus an unlimited partnership. If you are considering a partnership, take note that though a partnership agreement isn't mandatory, it is advisable, and obviously a written agreement is better than an oral one.

In contrast to a sole proprietorship or partnership, incorporating is a complex and costly affair and hence isn't recommended for small fledgling businesses. True, because a corporation is legally a separate entity if the business is sued, its assets are in jeopardy, not yours.* Also, a corporation has a better chance of getting financing and lines of credit with suppliers than does a sole proprietor, and obviously, you have to be a corporation (not just in business) to take advantage of corporate discounts. Unless you are competent enough to incorporate yourself, however, it can cost you several hundred to more than $1,000 to

---

*Before you get too excited about this, take note that the "corporate shield" is not bulletproof. If, for example, your business was wantonly undercapitalized or you haven't been on the up-and-up in your business dealings, a judge may rule that you are personally liable for the mistakes of your business.

start (for legal and filing fees) and possibly a few hundred a year to maintain. If you are interested in exploring incorporation, study up on "S" corporations as opposed to a regular corporation, known as "C" corporation. With a "C" Corporation you will be subject to double taxation on your profit: first on the corporation's profit (at the corporate tax, which is higher than the individual tax rate) and then on your income (or "dividends") from the business . The "S" Corporation (formerly known as "Subchapter S") is not subject to the double tax, but like the "C" Corporation it can cost you a pretty penny to start and maintain.

• **"Idea Care."** If you will have any "intellectual property"—an invention, a logo, your words—you should take steps to ensure that you'll have some legal protection for it, in the form of a patent, trademark, or copyright as appropriate. Even if you know you won't be applying for any of the above, it may be worth your while to know a little something about the subject to avoid inadvertently infringing upon someone else's turf. But let's assume that you have something that will need protection. What can you expect?

A patent gives you the exclusive rights to produce or sell an invention, a discovery of a process, or an improvement on something already in existence for fourteen or seventeen years, depending on what it is. For purposes of illustration, let's say you invent something called a Whatsit. Just because you've never seen it on the market doesn't mean it hasn't been conceived. To find out just how ingenious you have been, you need to hire a patent agent or attorney to conduct a search, which will turn up one of three things: (1) that there's a current or pending patent on all or part of the Whatsit, in which case the only way you can legally market it is if the inventor grants you a license; (2) that there's an expired patent on the item and hence it is in the public domain for anyone to profit from; or (3) that there's no current or expired patent, in which case you would then have to decide whether or not to just put it out on the market or file for a patent first. If you decide on patenting it, you should first have your Whatsit vetted by an invention-evaluation service (for referrals contact the nearest inventors' group). If you find that your invention is technically sound and commercially viable, then and only then should you proceed with the patent application. The reason is that securing a patent can cost you several thousand dollars in filing and legal fees and can take a few years to be finalized. For more information on patents and trademarks (discussed below) contact U.S. Department of Commerce, Patent and Trademark Office, Washington, DC 20231.

A trademark is a word, phrase, logo, symbol, design, or combination of all of these that identifies a certain product with a certain company. If you want to market your invention as "The Whatsit," as with the patent you will need to conduct a search. If you find that no one has a claim on your proposed trademark, you take possession of it by using it—that is, by having it on your letterhead, on your business cards, and in your advertisements, followed by the symbol ™ (for a product) or ℠ (for a service). If you want exclusive rights to it and full protection under the law you would have it registered. Hence, the symbol ®.

If you will be dealing in the written word, illustrations, or musical compositions and you don't have your work copyrighted, you won't have exclusive rights to its printing or reproduction. If you don't care about others using and possibly profiting off your creation without your permission, then you do not have to bother getting a copyright. If you do care, then you should print "copyright" or © and the year of creation on the work and register it with the Library of Congress. This involves filling out a form, paying a small fee (about $20), and submitting two copies of the work. For complete information, contact Register of Copyrights, Copyright Office, Library of Congress, Washington, DC 20559.

All these business matters may seem overwhelming, but

they really aren't *that* daunting—especially if you deal with them one at a time and well in advance of your actually getting down to the business of doing business. If you don't want to be bothered with these details, then you will have to pay someone to handle them for you—namely, an attorney who specializes in small business matters. If you're more intrepid, you'll save yourself a bundle in legal fees. But no matter how undaunted you are by legalese and bureaucrats, it's not a good idea to enter a business without at least one consultation with an attorney in order to make sure you haven't overlooked anything.

MAIL-ORDER FRAUD

Starting smart also means steering clear of fraud. As defined in the USPS booklet *A Consumer's Guide to postal Crime Prevention,* mail fraud is "a scheme to get money or anything of value from you by offering a product, service, or investment opportunity that does not live up to its claims." In everyday lingo, it's lying, cheating, and stealing. Some of the most blatant forms of fraud are:

- Failure to deliver prepaid merchandise.
- Failure to deliver a complete order without an explanation.
- Failure to honor the promise of a money-back guarantee.
- Failure to deliver merchandise that functions or appears as advertised.
- Bogus price claims. (You cannot offer something at a reduced price of $8 with the claim that the item formerly sold for $15 unless you have in actuality sold a fair amount of them at that price.)
- Bogus testimonials or endorsements.

This is not to suggest that there's such a thing as big fraud and little fraud, or that just because something you may be contemplating isn't among the top ten forms of fraud that you'll be able to get away with it. Fraud is fraud. And while many people have gotten away with major frauds, more than a few have been fined and put out of business (if not jailed) for what they considered a mere "white lie."

If you want to stay clean—and in business—it's really not that complicated. All you need do is abide by the Golden Rule: "Do unto others as you would have them do unto you." For the mail-order operator, this boils down to telling the truth and delivering the goods.

THE STANDARD OF EXCELLENCE

If the Golden Rule seems a little too vague and you don't trust your own sense of right and wrong, then you should study the Direct Marketing Association's pamphlet *Guidelines for Ethical Business Practices,* developed by the organization's Ethics and Consumer Affairs Department. The DMA is a networking, information, and advocacy organization for all varieties of direct marketers (for more on the DMA, see the Resource Guide). Their guidelines aren't law, but they do reflect the letter and spirit of the laws and the standards embraced by all direct marketers with a conscience. So if you abide by the DMA guidelines, it is highly unlikely that you will run afoul of the law or incur the wrath of your fellow mail-order operators. (Remember, honest direct marketers have a vested interest in blowing the whistle on the unscrupulous.) The time to acquaint yourself with the guidelines is *now*—that is, before you start your mail-order business—because doing so will enable you to make sounder decisions as you chart your course.

Here are the DMA guidelines reprinted in their entirety. Bear in mind that because the DMA is concerned with all manner of direct marketing, some of the articles may not now or ever apply to you as a mail-order operator.

THE DMA GUIDELINES FOR ETHICAL BUSINESS PRACTICES

THE TERMS OF THE OFFER

Honesty (Article #1): All offers should be clear, honest and complete so that the consumer may know the exact nature of what is being offered, the price, the terms of payment (including all extra charges), and the commitment involved in the placing of an order. Before publication of an offer, direct marketers should be prepared to substantiate any claims or offers made. Advertisements or specific claims which are untrue, misleading, deceptive, fraudulent or unjustly disparaging of competitors should not be used.

Clarity (Article #2): A simple statement of all the essential points of the offer should be clearly displayed in the promotional material. When an offer illustrates goods which are not included or cost extra, these facts should be made clear.

Print Size (Article #3): Print which by its small size, placement or other visual characteristics is likely to substantially affect the legibility of the offer, or exceptions to it should not be used.

Actual Conditions (Article #4): All descriptions and promises should be in accordance with actual conditions, situations and circumstances existing at the time of the promotion. Claims regarding any limitations (such as time or quantity) should be legitimate.

Disparagement (Article #5): Disparagement of any person or group on grounds of race, color, religion, national origin, sex, marital status, or age is unacceptable.

Standards (Article #6): Solicitations should not contain vulgar, immoral, profane, or offensive matter nor promote the sale of pornographic material or other matter not acceptable for advertising on moral grounds.

Advertising to Children (Article #7): Offers suitable for adults only should not be made to children.

Photographs and Art Work (Article #8): Photographs, illustrations, artwork, and the situations they represent should be accurate portrayals and current reproductions of the product, service, or other subject in all particulars.

Sponsor and Intent (Article #9): All direct marketing contacts should disclose the name of the sponsor and each purpose of the contact. No one should make offers or solicitations in the guise of research or a survey when the real intent is to sell products or services or to raise funds.

Identity of the Seller (Article #10): Every offer and shipment should sufficiently identify the name and street address of the direct marketer so that the consumer may contact the individual or company by mail or phone.

Solicitation in the Guise of an Invoice (Article #11): Offers that are likely to be mistaken as bills or invoices should not be used.

Postage and Handling Charges (Article #12): Postage or shipping charges and handling charges, if any, should reflect as accurately as practicable actual costs incurred.

SPECIAL OFFERS
Use of the Word "Free" and other Similar Representations (Article #13): A product or service which is offered without cost or obligation to the recipient may be unqualifiedly described as "free."

If a product or service is offered as "free," for a nominal cost or at a greatly reduced price and the offer requires the recipient to purchase some other product or service, all terms and conditions should be clearly and conspicuously disclosed and in close conjunction with the use of the term "free" or other similar phrase.

When the term "free" or other similar representations are made (for example, 2-for-1, half price or 1 cent offers), the product or service required to be purchased should not be increased in price or decreased in quality or quantity.

Negative Option Selling (Article #14): All direct marketers should comply with the FTC regulation governing Negative Option Plans. Some of the major requirements of this regulation are as follows:

Offers which require the consumer to return a notice sent by the seller before each periodic shipment to avoid receiving merchandise should contain all important conditions of the plan including.

a. A full description of the obligation to purchase a minimum number of items and all the charges involved, and

b. The procedures by which the consumer will receive the announcements of selections, and a statement of their frequency, as well as how to reject unwanted items, and how to cancel after completing the obligation.

The consumer should be given advance notice of the periodic selection so that the consumer may have a minimum of ten days to exercise a timely choice.

Because of the nature of this kind of offer, special attention should be given to the clarity, completeness, and prominent placement of the terms of the initial offering.

SWEEPSTAKES

Sweepstakes, as defined here, are promotional devices by which items of value (prizes) are awarded to participants by chance without the promoter's requiring them to render something of value to be eligible to participate (consideration). The co-existence of all three elements—prize, chance, and consideration—in the same promotion constitutes a lottery. It is illegal for any private enterprise to run a lottery.

When skill replaces chance, the promotion becomes a skill contest. When gifts (premiums or other items of value) are given to all participants independent of the element of chance, the promotion is not a sweepstakes and should not be held out as such.

Violations of the anti-lottery laws are policed and enforced at the federal level by the United States Postal Service, the Federal Communications Commission (when broadcast advertising is involved), and the Federal Trade Commission. Because sweepstakes are also regulated on a state-by-state basis, and the laws and definitions may vary by state, it is recommended that an attorney familiar with and experienced in the laws of sweepstakes be consulted before a sponsor conducts its promotion.

While this section of the Guidelines may focus on the promotional aspects of running a sweepstakes, it is equally important that the operation and administration of the sweepstakes be conducted in compliance with the ethical standards set forth in other selections as well.

Use of the Term "Sweepstakes" (Article #15): Only those promotional devices which specify the definition stated above should be called or held out to be sweepstakes.

No-Purchase Option (Article $16): The no-purchase option as well as the method for entering without ordering should be clearly disclosed. Response devices used only for entering the sweepstakes should be as visible as those utilized for ordering the product or service.

Prizes (Article #17): Sweepstakes prizes should be advertised in a manner that is clear, honest, and complete so that the consumer may know the exact nature of what is being offered.

Photographs, illustrations, artwork, and the situations they represent should be accurate portrayals of the prizes listed in the promotion.

No award should be held forth directly or by implication as having substantial monetary value if it is of nominal worth. The value of a prize given should be stated at a regular value, whether actual cost to the sponsor is greater or less.

Prizes should be delivered without cost to the participant. If there are certain conditions under which a prize or prizes will not be awarded, this fact should be disclosed in a manner that is easy to find and understand.

Premium (Article #18): If a premium, gift or item of value is offered by virtue of a participant's merely entering a sweepstakes, without any selection process taking place, it should be clear that everyone will receive it.

Chances of Winning (Article #19): No sweepstakes promotion, or any of its parts, should state or imply that a recipient has won a prize when this is not the case.

Winners should be selected in a manner that ensures fair application of the laws of chance.

Disclosure of Rules (Article #20): All terms and conditions of the sweepstakes, including entry procedures and rules, should be easy to find, read, and understand.

The following should be set forth clearly in the rules:
- No purchase of the advertised product or service is required in order to win a prize.
- Procedures for entry.
- If applicable, disclosure that a facsimile of the entry

blank or promotional device may be used to enter the sweepstakes.

- The termination date for eligibility in the sweepstakes. The termination date should specify whether it is a date of mailing or receipt of entry deadline.
- The number, retail value, and complete description of all prizes offered, and whether cash may be awarded instead of merchandise. If a cash prize is to be awarded by installment payments, that fact should be clearly disclosed, along with the nature and timing of the payments.
- The approximate odds of winning a prize or a statement that such odds depend on number of entrant.
- The method by which winners will be selected.
- The geographic area covered by the sweepstakes and those areas in which the offer is void.
- All eligibility requirements, if any.
- Approximate dates when winners will be selected and notified.
- Publicity rights re the use of winner's name.
- Taxes are the responsibility of the winner.
- Provision of a mailing address to allow consumers to submit a self-addressed, stamped envelope to receive a list of winners of prizes over $25.00 in value.

SPECIAL CLAIMS

Price Comparisons (Article #21): Price comparisons may be made in two ways:

a. between one's price and a former, future, or suggested price or

b. between one's price and the price of a competitor's comparable product.

In all price comparisons, the compared price against which the comparison is made must be fair and accurate.

In each case of comparison to a former, suggested or competitor's comparable product price, substantial sales should have been made at that price in the recent past.

For comparisons with a future price, there should be a reasonable expectation that the new price will be charged in the foreseeable future.

Guarantees (Article #22): If a product or service is offered with a "guarantee" or a "warranty," either the terms and conditions should be set forth in full in the promotion, or the promotion should state how the consumer may obtain a copy. The guarantee should clearly state the name and address of the guarantor and the duration of the guarantee.

Any requests for repair, replacement or refund under the terms of a "guarantee" or "warranty" should be honored promptly. In an unqualified offer of refund, repair or replacement, the customer's preference shall prevail.

Use of Test or Survey Data (Article #23): All test or survey data referred to in advertising should be competent and reliable as to source and methodology, and should support the specific claim for which it is cited. Advertising claims should not distort the test or survey results nor take them out of context.

Testimonials and Endorsements (Article #24): Testimonials and endorsements should be used only if they are:
   a. Authorized by the person quoted,
   b. Genuine and related to the experience of the person giving them and
   c. Not taken out of context so as to distort the endorser's opinion or experience with the product.

THE PRODUCT
Product Safety (Article #25): Products should be safe in normal use and be free of defects likely to cause injury. To that end, they should meet or exceed current, recognized health and safety norms and be adequately tested, where applicable. Information provided with the product should include proper directions for use and full

instructions covering assembly and safety warnings, whenever necessary.

Product Distribution Safety (Article #26): Products should be distributed only in a manner that will provide reasonable safeguards against possibilities of injury.

Product Availability (Article #27): Direct marketers should only offer merchandise when it is on hand or when there is a reasonable expectation of its receipt. Direct marketers should not engage in dry testing* unless the special nature of that offer is disclosed in the promotion.

FULFILLMENT
Unordered Merchandise (Article #28): Merchandise should not be shipped without having first received the customer's permission. The exceptions are samples or gifts clearly marked as such, and merchandise mailed by a charitable organization soliciting contributions, as long as all items are sent with a clear and conspicuous statement informing the recipient of an unqualified right to treat the product as a gift and to do with it as the recipient sees fit, at no cost or obligation to the recipient.

Shipments (Article #29): Direct marketers are reminded that they should abide by the FTC regulation regarding the prompt shipment of prepaid merchandise, the Mail Order Merchandise (Thirty-Day) Rule.

Beyond this regulation, direct marketers are urged to ship all orders as soon as possible.

CREDIT AND DEBT COLLECTION
Equal Credit Opportunity (Article #30): A creditor should not discriminate on the basis of race, color, religion, national origin, sex, marital status, or age. If an

---

*Dry testing is soliciting orders before you stock merchandise, the idea being to see what kind of demand there is for a product before you invest in inventory.

individual is rejected for credit, the creditor should be prepared to give reasons why.

Debt Collection (Article #31): Unfair, misleading, deceptive or abusive methods should not be used for collecting money. The direct marketer should take reasonable steps to assure that those collecting on the direct marketer's behalf comply with this guideline.

USE OF MAILING LISTS

List Rental Practices (Article #32): Consumers who provide data that may be rented, sold or exchanged for direct marketing purposes periodically should be informed of the potential for the rental, sale or exchange of such data. Marketers should offer an opportunity to have a consumer's name deleted or suppressed upon request.

List compilers should suppress names from lists when requested by the individual.

For each list that is to be rented, sold or exchanged, the DMA Mail Preference Service name-removal list and, when applicable, the DMA Telephone Preference Service name-removal list should be used. Names found on such suppression lists should not be rented, sold or exchanged, except for suppression purposes.

All persons involved in the rental, sale, or exchange of lists and data should take reasonable steps to ensure that industry members follow these guidelines.

Personal Information (Article #33): Direct marketers should be sensitive to the issue of consumer privacy and should limit the combination, collection, rental, sale, exchange and use of consumer data to only those data which are appropriate for direct marketing purposes.

Information and selection criteria that may be considered to be personal and intimate in nature by all reasonable standards should not provide the basis for lists made available for rental, sale, or exchange when there is a reasonable expectation by the consumer that the information will be kept confidential.

Any advertising or promotion for lists being offered for rental, sale, or exchange should reflect the fact that a list is an aggregate collection of marketing data. Such promotions should also reflect a sensitivity for the consumers on the those lists.

List Usage Agreements (Article #34): List owners, brokers, compilers, and users should make every attempt to establish the exact nature of the list's intended usage prior to the sale or rental of the list. Owners, brokers, and compilers should not permit the sale or rental of their lists for an offer that is in violation of any of the Ethical Guidelines of DMA. Promotions should be directed to those segments of the public most likely to be interested in their causes or to have a use for their products or services.

List Abuse (Article #35): No list or list data should be used in violation of the lawful rights of the list owner nor the agreement between the parties; any such misuse should be brought to the attention of the lawful owner.

TELEPHONE MARKETING
(See also Articles # 9 and #29)

Reasonable Hours (Article #36): All telephone contacts should be made during reasonable hours.

Taping of Conversations (Article #37): Taping of telephone conversations made for telephone marketing purposes should not be conducted without legal notice to or consent of all parties, or the use of a beeping device.

Telephone Name Removal/Restricted Contacts (Article #38): Telephone marketers should remove the name of any customer from their telephone lists when requested by the individual. Marketers should use the DMA Telephone Preference Service name-removal list and, when applicable, the Mail Preference Service name-removal list. Names found on such suppression lists should not be rented, sold, or exchanged, except for suppression purposes.

A telephone marketer should not knowingly call anyone who has an unlisted or unpublished telephone number, except in instances where the number was provided by the customer to that marketer.

Random dialing techniques, whether manual or automated, in which identification of the parties to be called is left to chance should not be used in sales and marketing solicitations.

Sequential dialing techniques, whether a manual or automated process, in which selection of those parties to be called is based on the location of their telephone numbers in a sequence of telephone numbers should not be used.

Disclosure and Tactics (Article #39): All telephone solicitations should disclose to the buyer, during the conversation, the cost of the merchandise, all terms, conditions and the payment plan, and whether there will be postage and handling charges. At no time should "high pressure" tactics be utilized.

Use of Automatic Electronic Equipment (Article #40): No telephone marketer should solicit sales using automatic electronic dialing equipment unless the telephone immediately disconnects when the called person hangs up.

FUND-RAISING
(See also Article #28)
Commission Prohibition/Authenticity of Organization (Article #41): Fund-raisers should make no percentage

or commission arrangements whereby any person or firm assisting or participating in a fund-raising activity is paid a fee proportionate to the funds raised, nor should they solicit for non-functioning organizations.

LAWS, CODES, AND REGULATIONS

(Article #42): Direct marketers should operate in accordance with the Better Business Bureau's Code of Advertising and be cognizant of and adhere to laws and regulations of the United States Postal Service, the Federal Trade Commission, the Federal Reserve Board, and other applicable federal, state and local laws governing advertising, marketing practices, and the transaction of business by mail, telephone, and the print and broadcast media.

Did you skim the Guidelines, or did you really read them? If you skimmed, you've done yourself a disservice. Remember, if you want to start off in the mail-order business on the right foot, it is imperative that you familiarize yourself with these tenets of ethical conduct. Whether you skimmed them or not, you should read them again and highlight the articles that obviously apply to mail-order selling. At this point no one would expect you to memorize the dos and don'ts discussed thus far, but you should process the information to the extent that if you move toward a "no-no" zone, an alarm will go off and you'll think to check into the legality or ethicality of the thing.

NINE

COUNTING
THE COST

As mentioned at the outset, one of the advantages of
a mail-order business is that it's a relatively low-
investment-and-quick-results business. If your initial advertising nets nothing or very little, you'll have the
option of cutting your losses and trying your hand at
something else or going back to the drawing board on your
product(s) or your advertising strategy, or both. If your
advertisements or direct-mail campaign pulls in big business, then you'll have plenty of time to expand your
operation and infrastructure. So until you've tested the
waters and have a quantifiable reason to believe your
mail-order business is viable, you should not sink a lot of
money into it. Start out slow, small, and as bare-bones as
possible.

In a few pages you'll find a Startup Chart that will help

you avoid underestimating how much you'll have to put out to start up. This chart lists the expenses most fledgling mail-order operators are likely to incur. But before you consider the essentials, review the following list of goods and services not found on the chart. These items range from somewhat to very useful to a mail-order operator, but they are not absolute musts. So you should only think of getting them if you can easily afford them and won't mind having them around in the event that your mail-order business fails to fly.

• **Personal Computer System.** A PC can be an absolute wonder worker when loaded with such time and money-saving software as word-processing, accounting, and graphics programs. There is also software specifically designed for mail-order businesses which facilitates all manner of record keeping and data processing, such as order entry, mailing-list management, accounts receivable, and inventory control. Two such programs worth checking out are *The Mail Order Wizard* (The Haven Corporation 802 Madison Street, Evanston, IL 60202; 800–782–8278; demo available for about $25) and *The Mail Order Accountant* (Goldsmith & Associates, 650 Santa Ray Avenue, Oakland, CA 94610; 510–444–7789; demo available for about $30).

If you are considering a computer, make a list of all the tasks you want to accomplish with it. Then research the software available for them and the kind and quality of hardware you'd need to run the various programs. If you aren't clear as to what you'll be doing with a computer, you run the risk of buying too little or too much machine—or worse, the wrong machine altogether.

Many people insist that a computer is an absolute necessity for a mail-order business. If it's a business that's up and running well and turning a profit, this is true. But for startup, a computer could wind up being a big regret. The hardware and software for a proper system could cost you several thousand dollars. So remember, if you can't borrow time on a friend's or relative's system, you can rent time at a computer center.

• **Printer.** An obvious must if you'll have a computer. If you intend to generate your own sales material, you should buy a laser printer as opposed to a dot-matrix or near-letter-quality one. With a laser printer you'll be able to generate a truly exquisite product.

• **Word processor.** If you are computer-phobic, you may want to consider a word processor to simplify such basic word work as correspondence.

• **Photocopier.** A time saver and a money saver if you don't have access to a copy center.

• **Postage meter.** Another device that saves time and money, because it ensures postage accuracy and eliminates trips to the post office for stamps (or waiting for them to arrive by mail). A bottom-of-the-line machine will have you taking the meter to the post office with a check for the amount you want to put in and having it filled. A top-of-the-line electronic meter can be filled over the phone (and you'll be billed). Pitney Bowes doesn't have a monopoly on the postage-meter business, but it is the main contender, with sales offices all around the country; for the one nearest you, consult the yellow pages for your area or contact Pitney Bowes World Headquarters at One Elmcroft, Stamford, CT 06926; (203) 356–5000. For others, consult your local business-to-business telephone directory, under "Mailing Machines & Equipment." By the way, postage meters are not for sale but for rent. The annual fee ranges from about $200 to $600.

• **Facsimile machine.** Necessary for communicating ASAP with your suppliers, professional service providers, and even customers (especially if you will be selling to businesses.)

- **Office furniture.** Since you won't have customers coming to your office, there's no need to dress your office for success. All that matters is that you are able to carry out comfortably the various tasks your business involves. So be creative. Use crates or boxes as file cabinets. Use the kitchen table or a card table as a work surface, unless of course you will have some heavy or delicate equipment (computer, printer, fax) that needs a sturdy and permanent resting place. When it comes to desktop tasks, the two most important purchases are a chair that will allow you to work at the proper height and give your back and lower body proper support, and good lighting, so that you can see what you're doing without strain.

- **Storage.** If your merchandise can rest safely and securely in a box, or several, in a corner or closet, then all you have to worry about is the actual storage space. If not, you may need to buy some shelving, a cabinet, or other kind of "home" for your goods.

- **Telephone.** If you have a busy and large household, a separate telephone for your business may be in order. Should you decide to get a another line, be forewarned that business service (installation and basic service) costs about three times more than residential service. Furthermore, business service requires a $300 deposit (even if your credit is A-1). What you get in exchange is a free straight-line listing in both the white and yellow pages for your area (and for an additional charge you can be listed in those of nearby counties or boroughs). Also, you can only place an ad in the yellow pages if you have business service. If you are toying with the idea of having an 800 number, take note that it may cost you at minimum about $20 per month (exclusive of the costs of the calls).

- **Answering machine.** A receptionist substitute, albeit only for incoming calls; but when you are your staff, every little bit helps. An answering machine is preferable to an answering service, because (barring mechanical failure) you'll get complete messages. Also, if you purchase a good machine, it'll be a one-time expense, whereas a service is a forever fee.

• **Post office box.** Many people assume they ought to have a post office box if they're going into the mail-order business, but "it ain't necessarily so." If you live in an area where mailbox break-ins are high or if mailbox overflow is likely to result in lost or stolen mail, then, yes, you have a valid reason to get one. But if you're motivated by a fear that the nosy will drop by your home to check you out, or the disgruntled to give you a piece of their mind, your energies are misplaced. Most mail-order shoppers aren't *that* curious about vendors, and if you treat people right no one will have reason to track you down. The other point you should bear in mind is that because fraud artists hide behind post office boxes, many people are leery about ordering from a company that only has a post office box, and many periodicals will not take an ad with a post office box. Both of these problems become nonproblems if you include your street address along with your post office box in your ad and on your stationery.

If you do decide to get a post office box, contact your local post office for information on fees, the application process, and box availability (if you live in a densely populated area the waiting list might be quite long, in which case you should get on it as soon as possible). If the waiting list is too long, check with private outfits like Mail Boxes Etc.

Now that you've had a chance to ponder the optional, take a look at those goods and services that are likely to be essentials. After you've reviewed the list, add any other goods and services you'll be needing or simply want to have. Then do a little thinking and a little research to get an estimate of the actual costs (plug in a zero for any item you do not need).

Startup Chart

ITEM	LOW	HIGH	ACTUAL
Permits/Licenses: Business license, resale certificate, fictitious-Name certificate, postal permits, etc.	$300	$500	_____
Inventory: Figure the cost of the least amount of merchandise with which you can start.			_____
Print Advertising: Multiply the cost of the number of ads you will run by the number of times you'll run them. If you will not be handling every aspect of ad development, be sure to include the cost for the services of a copywriter, illustrator, photographer, layout artist, etc.			_____
Direct-Mail Campaign: Your figure should include all production costs—from design to printing—as well as the cost of the mailing list(s) and postage.			_____
Typewriter: A must if you won't have a computer or word processor.	$200	$600	_____
Stationery: Letterhead, second sheets, business cards, envelopes. Remember, your stationery is your public face and people will consciously and subconsciously draw certain conclusions about your company based on it. The chintzier it is, the less enchanted people will be with you. The more gimmicky it is, the less people will trust you.	$200	$500	_____

Office Supplies: Be sure to include the cost of starter kits for any office equipment you add to this list—for example, toner for a printer; diskettes; and a surge protector for a computer. $100 $500   _____

Packaging and Mailing Supplies: For example, boxes, mailing bags, filler, mailing tape, mailing labels, scale. $100 $500

Research and Education: Books, periodicals, seminars, courses, and other audio and visual material. $300 $700   _____

Professional Services: Fees for consultations and/or work done by a business adviser, accountant, attorney, or advertising/marketing expert.   _____

Surprises: Inevitably there will be expenses that will take you by surprise, so it's a good idea to budget a little something for emergencies and oversights. $500 $1000   _____

_____   _____

_____   _____

_____   _____

_____   _____

_____   _____

_____   _____

Once you've counted the costs of getting into the mail-order business, you'll have a good idea of how soon it'll be before you will be financially able to start. If your projected startup costs come to several thousand dollars more than you have lying around, obviously you'll have to come up with a way of financing your enterprise. For this you can:

• **Save up.** Examine your spending habits and mend any extremely wasteful ways. Cut back on impulse buying. Give up one or more daily, weekly, monthly, or annual treats. If you are employed and have the option of paid overtime, take advantage of it, or find a part-time job. If you are unemployed but capable of holding down a full- or part-time job, hit the help-wanted ads. To chart your progress and keep yourself accountable, open a savings account for the money you garner from your newfound frugality and/or earnings.

AND/OR

• **Borrow.** Let this be your last resort. It's one thing to risk your savings, and another thing altogether to gamble with other people's money, which you'll have to pay back whether your business thrives or dives. So don't think too seriously about financing your business with borrowed money until you have neared the end of your research and preparation and feel confident that you do indeed know what you're doing. If and when you arrive at that point, you can do one or a combination of three things.

1. Take out a personal loan from a lending institution.
2. Plan to charge certain goods and services on your bank and/or store credit cards.
3. Take out a loan from a friend or relative (which is, by the way, how most small small businesses are financed). If this proves a viable option, for the sake of

your future relationship with the person, proceed with grace (don't push for an interest-free loan) and a realistic repayment plan.

Having the money to get started is only half the story. The other half—and perhaps the most important—is having a thorough understanding of exactly what you're getting into before you get into it.

TEN

RESOURCES

The first requirement for getting into the mail-order business is to educate yourself on the mail-order industry in general and the how-to of the various facets of the business, as well as the ins and outs, dos and don'ts, and ups and downs of being a home-based entrepreneur. Hence, the following list of people and publications that may prove helpful in your search for insight, information, and inspiration.

UNCLE SAM

U.S. Small Business Administration (SBA)
The SBA—which has offices in every state, the District of Columbia, the Virgin Islands, and Puerto Rico—was created

by Congress in 1953 to foster the growth and continuance of small businesses. It offers assistance in every aspect of starting and operating a business, from developing a business plan to securing capital. The following excerpts, from the pamphlet *Your Business & the SBA,* outlines some of the specific ways this government agency carries out its mandate:

- More than 13,000 volunteers in the **Service Corps of Retired Executives (SCORE)** provide training and one-on-one counseling at no charge.
- **Small Business Development Centers** provide training, counseling, and research at more than 600 locations nationwide.
- **Small Business Institutes** at more than 500 universities provide free management studies, performed by advanced business students under faculty direction.

When it comes to money matters, the SBA is not the first door you should knock on. By law, you must first apply to a bank or other lending institution before you turn to the SBA for financing assistance. The SBA financing program includes:

- **Small-loan guarantees,** to help businesses needing capital of $50,000 or less.
- **Small general-contractor loan guarantees,** for small construction businesses.
- **Seasonal line-of-credit guarantees,** for firms facing seasonal business increases.
- **Handicapped assistance loans,** for businesses owned by physically handicapped people and private nonprofit organizations that employ handicapped persons and operate in their interest.
- **Loans to disabled and Vietnam-era veterans** to start, operate, or expand a small business.

One of the most immediate ways the SBA assists novice entrepreneurs is through its numerous low-cost publications on everything from product and idea development to marketing. Those of particular interest to the would-be mail-order operator include *Ideas into Dollars; Researching Your Market; The Business Plan for Home-Based Business; Avoiding Patent, Trademark and Copyright Problems; Selecting the Legal Structure of Your Business; Pricing Your Products and Services Profitably; Record Keeping in a Small Business; Should You Lease or Buy Equipment?; Inventory Management; Advertising;* and *Selling by Mail Order.*

For the SBA office nearest you, consult the "U.S. Government Offices" section (the blue pages) in your telephone directory. For a free catalogue of SBA publications and videos write: Small Business Directory, P.O. Box 1000, Fort Worth, TX 76119.

Federal Trade Commission (FTC)

This regulatory agency exists to support the workings of our free market economy and protect the buying public from unfair methods of competition. You can study up on the ABCs of the FTC and its impact on a mail-order business through the following free publications: *A Business Guide to the FTC's Mail Order Rule, A Guide to the Federal Trade Commission,* and *What's Going on at the FTC?* You can request these from the FTC headquarters at 6th and Pennsylvania Avenue, NW, Washington, D.C. 20580; (202) 326-2222; or at one of its ten regional offices in the following cities: Atlanta, Boston, Chicago, Cleveland, Dallas, Denver, Los Angeles, New York, San Francisco, and Seattle.

United States Postal Service (USPS)

USPS has a number of free publications with tips on making the most of our mail system and information on its various services. Among them: *A Guide to Business Mail Preparation, Postal Addressing Standards, How to Prepare and Wrap Packages, Third-Class Mail Preparation,* and *Information Guide on Presort First-Class Mail.* If these publications are not available at your local post office, contact the G.P.O. (general post office) for your area. If you cannot get satisfaction here contact USPS headquarters at 475 L'Enfant Plaza, SW, Washington, DC 20260. USPS also puts out a monthly bulletin, *Memo to Mailers,* on changes in postal regulations, rates, and operating procedures. For this you must write to Memo for Mailers, USPS, P.O. Box 999, Springfield, VA 22150-0999.

Government Printing Office (GPO)

The government is an overlooked source of literally thousands and thousands of books, pamphlets, and periodicals on almost every subject under the sun—from "Accidents and Accident Prevention" to "Landscape Gardening" and "Yearbooks." The must publication for a mail-order business is the annual *Domestic Mail Manual* (about $40), which contains up-to-date information on postal rates, regulations, and other mail matters.

Because the GPO has an inventory of over 15,000 titles, it does not publish a comprehensive catalogue of all available titles. Instead, there are catalogues for individual subject categories. These are called Subject Bibliographies, and there are over two hundred of them. Subject Bibliographies, like the Subject Bibliography Index in which they are all listed, are free. For a Subject Bibliography Index and/or the U.S. Government Bookstore nearest you, contact U.S. Government Printing Office, Superintendent of Documents, Washington, DC 20402; 202-512-0000 or 202-783-3238.

Consumer Information Center

This agency stocks hundreds of free and low-cost publications of various federal agencies, including the Department of Commerce, the FTC, the SBA, and the USPS, and as such is an alternative source for many of the publications mentioned here, as well as others that may prove useful. For a free catalogue contact Consumer Information Center, P.O. Box 100, Pueblo, CO 81002; 719-948-3334.

Federal Information Center

"Have you ever tried to find an answer to a simple question about the federal government and ended up on a merry-go-round of referrals? Or have you ever had a question about the federal government that was so difficult that you didn't even know where to begin?" asks the U.S. General Services Administration in its FIC pamphlet. Anticipating an anguished "Yes!," it goes on to add: "The Federal Information Center is one office that has specially selected and trained its staff to answer your questions or help you find the right person with the answer." Consult the "U.S. Government Offices" section of your telephone directory for the Federal Information Center 800 number for your metropolitan area or state, call 301-722-9098, or write to the FIC at P.O. Box 600, Cumberland, MD 21502. Users of Telecommunications Devices for the Deaf (TDD/TTY) may call 800-326-2996 from any point in the United States.

State Information Center

This is where you call for questions specific to your state. For the number, contact the Federal Information Center, or call directory assistance in your state capital.

Internal Revenue Service

Believe it or not, you do have a friend in the IRS—that is, when it comes to accessing information on how to stay on its good side. The IRS publishes a number of free publications to, as they say, "make your taxes less taxing." Even if you plan to use a tax preparer or accountant, it doesn't hurt to know a little something yourself. Some of the IRS booklets of particular interest to the entrepreneur are *Tax Guide for Small Business* (#334); *Business Use of Your Home* (#587); *Business Use of Your Car* (#917); *Depreciation* (#534); *Self-Employment Income and Tax* (#533); *Retirement Plans for the Self-Employed* (#560); *Business Expenses* (#535); and *Guide to Free Tax Services* (#910), which includes a list of all free publications. For these and other free publications, write Forms Distribution Center,

P.O. Box 25866, Richmond, VA 23260; or call 800-829-3676, which spells 800-TAX-FORM.

ORGANIZATIONS

Direct Marketing Association (DMA)

This networking, resource, and advocacy organization is the largest professional organization in the field of direct marketing. Membership, which starts at about $500, includes access to DMA's Library & Resource Center (the largest database of direct marketing facts, figures, theories, and case histories), as well as discounts on group medical insurance, books, reports, DMA conferences, and seminars (for example, "Catalog Basics," "The Law and Direct Marketing," "Winning Direct Mail"), among other services. Members also receive (free) three DMA publications: *Washington Update* (monthly) and *Washington Report* (bi-weekly), for news on legislative and regulatory issues, and *Direct Line,* a monthly report card on the DMA's activities. For more information contact DMA headquarters at 11 West 42nd Street, New York, NY 10036-8096; 212-768-7277.

National Association for the Self-Employed (NASE)

This organization of 300,000+ members is the oldest and largest association of small-time operators. Membership (about $70) includes discounts on group medical insurance, a range of products and services, and its newsletter, *Self-Employed America.* For more information contact NASE at 2121 Precinct Line Road, Suite 100, Hurst, TX 76054; (800) 232-NASE.

PERIODICALS

The following list of mail-order and small business-interest magazines and newsletters may be useful as advertising

venues as well as sources of information, inspiration, and
networking opportunities. All prices are for one-year subscriptions.

Direct Marketing (monthly magazine; $52). 224 Seventh
    Street, Garden City, NY 11530.
Entrepreneur: The Small Business Authority (monthly
    magazine; $19.97). P.O. Box 50368, Boulder, CO
    80321-0368; 800-421-2300 (from outside of Colorado),
    800-352-7449 (in Colorado).
Extra Income (bimonthly magazine; $11.95). P.O. Box 543,
    Mt. Morris, IL 61054.
Home-Office Computing (monthly magazine; $16.97). P.O.
    Box 2511, Boulder, CO 80302; 800-288-7812.
*Home Sweet Home: The Magazine for Families Who Make
    the Home Their Business* (quarterly; $20). E. 201
    Bourgault Road, Shelton, WA 98584; 206-427-7173.
*Homework: The Home Business Newsletter with a Christian
    Perspective* (bimonthly; $20). P.O. Box 394, Dept. LMP,
    Simsbury, CT 06070.
*Mail Profit™: "The How-to-Make-Money-by-Mail Maga-
    zine"* (bimonthly; $15 for third-class delivery, $25 for
    first-class delivery). P.O. Box 4785, Lincoln, NE 68504.
Mail Order Messenger (bimonthly in newspaper format:
    $12). P.O. Box 358, Middleton, TN 38052.
National Home Business Report (quarterly newsletter; $24).
    P.O. Box 2137, Naperville, IL 60567. Published by
    Barbara Brabec, who has been working from her
    home for over twenty years and ranks among the
    leading authorities in the home-based business indus-
    try.
Working from Home (monthly newsletter; $60). P.O. Box
    1722, Hallandale, FL 33008; 800-238-3008.

No matter the nature or the size of your business, as an
entrepreneur you should keep up with what's going on in
the business world at large by reading such general business periodicals as *Business Week, Forbes, Fortune, Barron's:*

The National Business and Financial Weekly, and the *Wall Street Journal.* For additional business periodicals, consult the *Readers' Guide to Periodical Literature* and the *Business Periodicals Index* at your local library.

BOOKS

The following titles represent a very small percentage of the books on mail-order, home-based entrepreneuring, and miscellaneous business matters in general. For a gander at the whole nine yards, consult the subject guide of *Books in Print* at your local library.

On Mail Order in General

Building a Mail Order Business: A Complete Manual for Success (3d edition), by William Cohen. John Wiley & Sons, 1991. One of the most comprehensive and engaging books on the subject.

How to Start and Operate a Mail-Order Business (5th edition), by Julian L. Simon. McGraw-Hill, 1993.

Home-Based Mail Order: A Success Guide for Entrepreneurs, by William J. Bond. Liberty Hall Press, 1990.

How I Made $1,000,000 in Mail Order, by Joseph E. Cossman. Simon & Schuster, 1984.

How to Build a Multi-Million Dollar Catalog Mail Order Business by Someone Who Did, by Lawson Traphagen Hill. Simon & Schuster, 1984.

How to Make Money in Mail-Order, by L. Perry Wilbur. John Wiley & Sons, 1990.

Mail Order Know-How, by Cecil Hoge. Ten Speed Press, 1992.

Mail Order Legal Manual (2d edition), by Erwin J. Keup. The Oasis Press, 1993.

Mail Order Moonlighting, by Cecil Hoge. Ten Speed Press, 1988.

Mail Order Product Guide, by Barry Klein. Todd Publications, 1989. A listing of more than 1,500 manufacturers, importers, and distributors of mail-order-appropriate products.

Mail Order Selling Made Easier, by John Kremer. Open Horizons Publishing Co., 1990.

Money in Your Mailbox: How to Start and Operate a Mail-Order Business (2d edition), by L. Perry Wilbur. John Wiley & Sons, 1992.

The Solid Gold Mailbox, by Walter H. Weintz. John Wiley & Sons, 1987.

On Advertising and Direct-Marketing Matters

Advertising Pure and Simple, by Hank Seiden. AMACOM, 1990.

The Complete Direct Mail List Handbook, by Ed Burnett. Prentice-Hall, 1988. A comprehensive guide on every aspect of mailing lists, from procurement to testing to list maintenance.

Direct Mail Copy That Sells, by Herschell Gordon Lewis. Prentice-Hall, 1984.

Do-It-Yourself Advertising: How to Produce Great Ads, Catalogs, Direct Mail and Much More, by Fred Hahn. John Wiley & Sons, 1992.

Do-It-Yourself Direct Marketing, by Mark S. Bacon. John Wiley & Sons, 1992.

Great Print Advertising: Creative Approaches, Strategies and Tactics, by Anthony L. Antin. John Wiley & Sons, 1993.

Inside the Leading Mail Order Houses (3d edition), by Maxwell Sroge. NTC Publishing Group, 1989.

More Than You Ever Wanted to Know about Mail Order Advertising, by Herschell G. Lewis. Prentice-Hall, 1983.

NTC's Dictionary of Direct Mail and Mailing List Terminology and Techniques, by Nat G. Bodian. NTC Publishing Group, 1991.

Power Direct Marketing, by Ray Jutkins. NTC Publishing Group, 1993.

Successful Direct Marketing Methods (5th edition), by Bob Stone. NTC Publishing Group, 1993. Regarded by many as *the* book on direct marketing.

Tested Advertising Methods (4th edition), by John Caples. Prentice-Hall, 1980.

Which Ad Pulled Best? (7th edition), by Philip Ward Burton and Scott C. Purvis. NTC Publishing Group, 1993.

On Money Matter and Miscellaneous Business Affairs

Basic Accounting for the Small Business, by Clive G. Cornish. TAB Books, 1981.

Keeping the Books: Basic Recordkeeping and Accounting for the Small Business (2d edition), by Linda Pinson and Jerry Jinnett. Dearborn Trade, 1993.

Free Money for Small Businesses and Entrepreneurs (3d edition), by Laurie Blum. John Wiley & Sons, 1992.

Government Giveaways for Entrepreneurs (2d edition), by Matthew Lesko. Information USA, 1989. Some 9,000 sources of federal and state money.

Guerilla Financing: Alternative Techniques to Finance any Small Business, by Bruce Blechman and Jay Conrad Levinson. Houghton Mifflin, 1991.

1,001 Ways to Cut Your Expenses, by Jonathan D. Pond. Dell, 1992.

Starting on a Shoestring: Building a Business Without a Bankroll (2d edition), by Arnold S. Goldstein. John Wiley & Sons, 1991.

Inventing & Patenting Sourcebook (biennial). Gale Research. 1,000+ page how-to guide and directory for getting your idea off the drawing board and into the marketplace.

Patent it Yourself (3rd edition), by David Pressman. Nolo Press, 1992.

Trademark: How to Name Your Business and Product, by Kate McGarth and Stephen Elias. Nolo Press, 1992.

How to Form Your Own Corporation Without a Lawyer for Under $75 (20th anniversary edition), by Ted Nicholas. Dearborn Trade, 1992.

Inc. Yourself: How to Profit by Setting Up Your Own Corporation (7th edition), by Judith H. McQuown. HarperCollins, 1992.

Starting Your Subchapter "S" Corporation (2d edition), by Arnold S. Goldstein and Robert L. Davidson III. John Wiley & Sons, 1992.

The Small Business Partnership Kit, by Robert L. Davidson III. John Wiley & Sons, 1992.

How to Really Create a Successful Business Plan, by David E. Gumpert. Inc. Publishing, 1990.

How to Write a Business Plan (3d edition), by Mike McKeever. Nolo Press, 1988.

On the Home-Based Business in General

The Home-Based Entrepreneur: The Complete Guide to Working at Home (2d edition), by Linda Pinson and Jerry Jinnett. Dearborn Trade, 1993.

Home Business→Big Business: How to Launch Your Home Business and Make It a Success, by Mel Cook. Collier Books, 1992.

Homemade Business: A Woman's Step-by-Step Guide to Earning Money at Home, by Donna Partow. Focus on the Family Publishing, 1992.

Homemade Money: The Definitive Guide to Success in a Home Business (4th edition), by Barbara Brabec. Betterway Publications, 1992.

Making It on Your Own: Surviving and Thriving on the Ups

and Downs of Being Your Own Boss, by Paul and Sarah Edwards. Jeremy P. Tarcher, 1991.

Starting a Business in Your Home, by Tonya Bolden. Longmeadow Press, 1993.

Starting & Operating a Home-Based Business, by David R. Eyler. John Wiley & Sons, 1989.

Working at Home, by Lindsey O'Connor. Harvest House, 1990.

Working for Yourself: Full Time, Part Time, Anytime, by Joseph Anthony. Kiplinger Books, 1992.

Working from Home: Everything You Need to Know About Living and Working Under the Same Roof (3d edition), by Paul and Sarah Edwards. Jeremy P. Tarcher, 1991.

If you enjoyed this No Nonsense Guide you may want to order these other No Nonsense Guides:

ITEM No.	TITLE	PRICE
0681401257	Starting A Business in Your Home	4.95
0681413891	How to Re-enter The Work Force	4.95
0681410450	How To Choose a Career	4.95

Ordering is easy and convenient.
Order by phone with Visa, MasterCard, American Express or Discover:
☎ **1-800-322-2000,** Dept. 706
or send your order to:
Longmeadow Press, Order/Dept. 706,
P.O. Box 305188, Nashville, TN 37230-5188

Name _____
Address _____
City _____ State _____ Zip _____

Item No.	Title	Qty	Total

Check or Money Order enclosed Payable to Longmeadow Press — **Subtotal**

Charge: ❏ MasterCard ❏ VISA ❏ American Express ❏ Discover — **Tax**

Account Number — **Shipping** — 2.95

☐☐☐☐☐ ☐☐☐☐☐ ☐☐☐☐☐ ☐☐☐☐☐ — **Total**

Card Expires

☐☐☐☐☐

Signaure _____ Date _____

Please add your applicable sales tax: AK, DE, MT, OR, 0.0%—CO, 3.8%—AL, HI, LA, MI, WY, 4.0%—VA. 4.5%—GA, IA, ID, IN, MA, MD, ME, OH, SC, SD, VT, WI, 5.0%—AR, AZ, 5.5%—MO, 5.725%—KS, 5.9%—CT, DC, FL, KY, NC, ND, NE, NJ, PA, WV, 6.0%—IL, MN, UT, 6.25%—MN, 6.5%—MS, NV, NY, RI, 7.0%—CA, TX, 7.25%—OK, 7.5%—WA. 7.8%—TN, 8.25%